Music in the Primary School

Oxford Music Education Series

The *Oxford Music Education Series* was established with Janet Mills (1954–2007) as series editor to present concise, readable, and thought-provoking handbooks for all those involved in music education, including teachers, community musicians, researchers, policy-makers, and parents/carers. The series encompasses a wide range of topics and musical styles, and aims to provide 'food for thought' for all those looking to broaden their understanding and further develop their work. Written by acknowledged leaders of education who are passionate about their subject, the books present cutting-edge ideas and aim to stimulate good practice by showing the practical implications of research.

Other titles in the Oxford Music Education Series

Janet Mills: *Music in the School* (2005)

Janet Mills: *Instrumental Teaching* (2007)

Adam Ockelford: *Music for Children and Young People with Complex Needs* (2008)

John Paynter and Janet Mills (eds): *Thinking and Making: Selections from the Writings of John Paynter on music in education* (2008)

David Bray: *Creating a Musical School* (2009)

Music in the Primary School

THIRD EDITION

Janet Mills

MUSIC DEPARTMENT

OXFORD
UNIVERSITY PRESS

OXFORD

UNIVERSITY PRESS

Great Clarendon Street, Oxford OX2 6DP, England

198 Madison Avenue, New York, NY 10016, USA

Oxford University Press is a department of the University of Oxford.
It furthers the University's aim of excellence in research, scholarship, and
education by publishing worldwide in

Oxford New York

Auckland Cape Town Hong Kong Karachi
Kuala Lumpur Madrid Melbourne Mexico City
Nairobi New Delhi Shanghai Taipei Toronto

With offices in

Argentina Austria Brazil Chile Czech Republic France Greece
Guatemala Hungary Italy Japan Poland Portugal Singapore
South Korea Switzerland Thailand Turkey Ukraine Vietnam

Oxford is a registered trade mark of Oxford University Press in the UK and
in certain other countries

Foreword © John Paynter 1991, 2009
Preface to this edition © Lis McCullough 2009
This edition © The Estate of Janet Mills 2009

Janet Mills has asserted her right under the Copyright, Designs and Patents
Act, 1988, to be identified as Author of this Work

Database right Oxford University Press (maker)

First published by Cambridge University Press 1991
Second Edition published by Cambridge University Press 1993
This edition first published by Oxford University Press 2009

British Library Cataloguing-in-Publication Data

Data available

Library of Congress Cataloging-in-Publication Data

Mills, Janet.
  Music in the primary school / Janet Mills. – 3rd ed.
    p. cm. – (Oxford music education series)
    ISBN 978-0-19-336495-0
  1. Music–Instruction and study.   2. School music–Instruction and
study   I. Title
    MT1.M626 2009
    372.87–dc22   2009019328

10 9 8 7 6

Typeset by RefineCatch Limited, Bungay, Suffolk
Printed in Great Britain by Ashford Colour Press Ltd

Preface to the Third Edition

When the original edition of *Music in the Primary School* was published in 1991 it was immediately popular with classroom teachers and with those involved in initial teacher education. Its great strength, then and now, is the multi-level content involving a mix of practical classroom suggestions, underlying pedagogical principles, and research findings. This interwoven material reflects and draws on the author's wide range of professional experiences, being firmly rooted in practice and very much on the side of generalist teachers in school, whatever their own musical experience and expertise. This point was highlighted in John Paynter's Foreword to the original edition, which is reproduced here. Paynter reflects on the earlier assumption that the ideal music teacher was an accomplished pianist, whereas the paramount requirement is, in fact, confidence. He describes how, through the underlying insistence that music is for *everyone* and that each teacher can do *something*, Janet Mills provides a realistic framework for the class teacher—the person best placed to embed music within a child's education.

The 1993 edition of *Music in the Primary School* took account of the introduction of the National Curriculum for Music in England. However, since then there have been changes in National Curriculum requirements for all subjects and a host of new initiatives across the education field, including many involving music. An update to this standard text is therefore to be welcomed, not least as a timely reminder of the fundamental principles of good practice. In addition, there are insightful new sections on the musical development of pre-school children and of teachers, and on the possibility of whether music can 'improve the mind'. During the course of this latest edition Janet justifies reference to the booklet *Music from 5–16* (DES, 1985) by describing it as 'timeless, visionary, and thoroughly musical'. The same description could equally apply to *Music in the Primary School*.

Most of us involved in music education have been lucky enough to benefit from Janet's influence, consciously or not; some were also lucky enough to be her friends. Janet worked on this edition during 2007 and it was the last major publication she completed before her untimely death at the end of that year.

When reading this book one hears her voice, and thus this edition is a reminder of Janet herself: her commitment, wisdom, pragmatism, and integrity as she promoted—in academic, government, and classroom arenas—the music making of pupils and teachers.

Lis McCullough
Chair of the National Association of Music Educators 2008–09

Foreword

Time was when most application forms for teaching posts in primary schools included the question 'Do you play the piano?' It usually came right at the end; you were never quite sure why. Was it an afterthought—suggesting that music had no great significance in the curriculum, but it would be useful to have someone who could play the hymns for assembly? Or was it a last, desperate cry from the heart—'We hardly dare mention this, but if you should just happen to play the piano that would be marvellous. You can take every class for singing, and you can organize the Christmas concert, and play for country dancing; and, because you obviously know how to read music, you can teach recorders and organize a percussion band ... and ... and ... Someone who could play the piano was the answer to many a headteacher's prayers.

In the expectation that only a minority of applicants would answer that question in the affirmative, schools looked to the teacher training colleges (as they were then called) to put on 'curriculum courses' that would equip teachers to cope with their own class music lessons. But here again, the norm against which the course content was measured was still the accomplished piano-playing teacher; in some way students were to be brought as close as possible to that ideal, even though the time allocated was not normally more than a few hours a week across a single academic year. Lecturers tried hard to encourage and inspire, and students—beginner pianists, elementary recorder players, first-position violinists—laboured bravely to reach worthwhile standards and to acquire repertoires for singing and music appreciation lessons. But the one thing such curriculum courses could not guarantee to deliver was the confidence needed to teach music.

Janet Mills assumes that 'Music is for all teachers' but she does not assume that every teacher has to be a pianist. The strength of her argument is its realistic approach; there must be something that everyone can do. But confidence is paramount. Accepting that music now has a high priority in primary schools and is endorsed by the National Curriculum, this book sets out a comprehensive scheme that really can be organized and taught by the generalist teacher.

No longer do we regard music in schools as icing on the cake; and it should now be clear that few people are better placed than primary-school class teachers to see that musical experience becomes, from the start, a truly important part of every child's education.

John Paynter

About the author

Janet Mills read music and mathematics at the University of York, followed by a PGCE at the University of Leeds. She then became Head of Music at The Holy Family School in Keighley, and later at Brighouse Girls' Grammar School. After a D.Phil at the University of Oxford she took up lecturing posts at Westminster College, Oxford and the University of Exeter, working mainly with aspiring and serving primary teachers. From 1990 to 2000 she was an HM Inspector of Schools working in all aspects of education, and she was Ofsted's specialist adviser for music from 1995. In 2000 she became a Research Fellow at the Royal College of Music in London, a post she held until her death in 2007.

Janet Mills was author of *Music in the School* (2005), *Instrumental Teaching* (2007), and many articles in books, magazines and research journals, as well as being founding editor of the Oxford Music Education Series. She was a major international figure in the world of music education, bringing a rare combination of razor-sharp intellect, impish sense of humour and vast practical experience, for she worked in various capacities in over 800 primary, secondary, and special schools. In 2004 she was awarded a National Teaching Fellowship for her 'outstanding contributions to teaching and learning'.

Acknowledgements

I wish to thank all the teachers and student teachers who helped with the development of this book. I owe a particular debt of gratitude to Sally Crane, Sally Crowther, Poppy Hughes, and Wendy Reynolds.

In connection with this new edition, special thanks are due to Lis McCullough. I am also very grateful to Margaret Barrett, Karen Brock, Sue Cottrell, Leonora Davies, Sarah Hennessy, Diane Price, and Mary Worthington.

I wish to thank Philip Croydon, his predecessor Kristen Thorner, and the music staff at Oxford University Press for their tremendous enthusiasm and support for this new edition.

David Acheson and Jennifer Buckham took the photographs, and I would like to thank Miss Winifred Pope, Headteacher at Wantage CE Junior School, and Miss Eileen Mann, Acting Headteacher at SS Mary and John CE First School, Oxford, for permitting those photographs to be taken in their schools.

Last, but far from least, the children. Some appear in case studies, and others in photographs. But many more have, sometimes unwittingly, played their part in the development of my ideas. I wish to thank them all.

Contents

Photographs, figures, and table

Photographs

Figures

Table

Copyright acknowledgements

Pages
16, 24–5,
30–1, 70–1   Photographs by David Acheson. Reproduced by permission.
141–2   Janet Mills, 'Reponse to Katie Overy's paper, "Can we really improve the mind" ', *Psychology of Music*, Society for Education, Music and Psychological Research, 1998. First published by SAGE Publications Ltd.
143   Janet Mills, 'In defence of auditory learning', *Link Magazine*, 1998
101   Keith Swanwick and June Tillman, 'The sequence of musical development: a study of children's composition', *British Journal of Music Education* **3**/3, Cambridge University Press, 1986

Every effort has been made to seek permission for the use of all copyright items in this book. In the event that any item has been overlooked, the publishers will be glad to rectify this on reprint.

Abbreviations

A level Advanced level (General Certificate of Education) (national examinations taken typically by 18-year-olds)

APMT Association of Professional Music Therapists

CACE Central Advisory Council for Education

DES Department of Education and Science

DfEE Department for Education and Employment

GCSE General Certificate of Secondary Education (national examinations taken typically by 16-year-olds)

HMI Her Majesty's Inspectorate/Inspector(s)

ICT Information and Communication Technology

NAME National Association of Music Educators

NFER National Foundation for Educational Research

QCA Qualifications and Curriculum Authority

SEN Special educational needs

Chapter 1

Primary teachers and music

I am more concerned for the future of the human race than I am for the future of music.

Richard Addison in *Beyond Music* (Addison 1988: 13)

Music education should be mainly concerned with bringing pupils into contact with the musician's fundamental activities of performing, composing and learning.

HM Inspectorate in *Curriculum Matters 4: Music from 5 to 16*
(DES 1985: 2)

I have to say, in the end, I think that all that matters in music education is that what we do is musical [i.e. of music]. I don't care what it is. I would applaud whatever was happening in a classroom provided that it was actually involving pupils in musical experience.

John Paynter, in W. Salaman, 'Personalities in World Music Education'
(Salaman 1988: 13)

Music in primary schools

I start by outlining my view of the place of music in primary schools. Like Richard Addison, I think that music education has more to do with the education of pupils than the transmission of some musical heritage, however defined. Like the writers of *Music from 5 to 16*, I think of music education as an active experience in which pupils compose, perform, and listen. Like John Paynter, I want pupils actually to do music during music lessons, and I do not feel that there is a canon of music that everyone—pupil or teacher—should learn. I believe that the values and principles that Richard Addison, HM Inspectors, and John Paynter, amongst others, expounded in the late 1980s were those upon which the National Curriculum for music in England and Wales was built, and has been developed subsequently. I believe also that these values and principles would underpin any sensible music education anywhere, and at any time, whether or not there was a National Curriculum in place.

Not all activities that sometimes pass for music in primary school are, in my terms, music. Drawing a flute is not music, though it might be an appropriate artistic activity for pupils who have just performed the musical activity of listening to a flute being played. Reading about the life of Mozart is not music, though it could be a useful language exercise for pupils who have listened to a piece by Mozart, and who want to find out more about his life. Making a musical instrument is not music, though playing it may be. Learning to operate a piece of computer software is not music, but using it to enhance composing or performing is a thoroughly musical activity.

The activities of composing, performing, and listening are fundamental to musicianship, and practice in them may result in some pupils ultimately choosing careers in music, for example as jazz musician, composer, critic, or music teacher. But I do not engage primary pupils in composing, performing, and listening out of any vocational motive—rather because I want them to grow through music. All pupils can grow through music, so music education is for all pupils.

As music is for all pupils, the music curriculum must be determined in response to individual musical need. No single blanket programme will be suitable for all pupils, any more than it would be in mathematics or English. No special group, for instance, those, sometimes referred to as gifted or talented, who will become able performers, has any higher claim on the music curriculum. All pupils have an equal right to an appropriate music education.

Music is for all teachers. I mean by this that primary pupils ideally do most, if not all, of their music with their class teacher, not a specialist teacher who sees them only for music. In the past, many primary schools employed teachers who teach only music—sometimes known as music specialists—to take responsibility for the music of several classes. This contrasted with practice in all other curriculum areas where classes are taught usually by class teachers on the grounds that the advantages of having a teacher who knows you outweighs those of being taught by someone with particular specialist expertise (Mills 1995/6). If this is true of other areas, why is it not true of music? In practice, music is often perceived as being different because music teachers are assumed to need skills that it would be unreasonable to expect all teachers to possess. Music lessons are sometimes organized rather like rehearsals of choirs and orchestras, with the teacher conducting, playing piano or guitar, and demonstrating on a range of instruments, including her singing voice. In this sort of lesson, the teacher does need to be in musical control. But, as we shall see later, there is no need to organize music lessons like this. Just as we can develop pupils' written language without being a novelist, it is perfectly possible to engage pupils in music without being a pianist. Of course, having specialist music skills is useful to teachers, and schools will still need teachers who can play the piano or keyboard, direct choirs, and so forth. But there is no need for these people to do all the music teaching in the school. Class teachers, given appropriate preparation and support, are all capable of teaching music. This way, music takes its place as part of the whole primary curriculum. Pupils and teachers make day-to-day links between work in music and other curriculum areas. Class teachers who have traditionally accepted full responsibility for the progress of each pupil in their class will know their pupils' musical progress at first hand.

Finally, music in the primary school must be an activity that is pleasurable for both pupils and teachers. I do not mean to suggest that music should be organized solely as entertainment, or that the atmosphere in a music lesson should always be akin to that of a party. In any case, that would be unlikely to result in pleasure for the teacher. I mean that the process of working as a musician—by composing, performing, and listening—must be enjoyable if it is to have any value. Similarly, the business of facilitating the musical activity of pupils must be pleasurable and satisfying for the teacher. Music lessons that become boring, which degenerate into disciplinary incidents, or which culminate in the teacher haranguing the class about extra-musical matters, such as holding books properly, paying attention, and sitting up straight, are worse than useless. Pupils who repeatedly attend this sort of music lesson become disenchanted with music long before they enter secondary school. Of course there will be moments in music lessons when a pupil has to be reprimanded. There will be occasions when pupils must be encouraged to increase the standards they set for their work in music. This might even mean asking pupils to revisit work they rather hoped was finished. But music should be something we engage in because we feel better for it. If should never become a mere duty, for teachers or pupils.

In short, music is

◆ an active subject consisting of the activities of composing, performing, and listening
◆ for all pupils
◆ for all teachers
◆ fun.

Primary music teachers

I have said that music is a subject for all teachers. Yet there are, at present, many primary teachers who are reluctant to teach music. There is nothing new about this. Research[1] (DES 1978) carried out before the National Curriculum was introduced showed that music was the subject in which pupils were most likely to be taught by someone other than their class teacher. In 1983[2] it was also the subject that fewest teachers thought they needed to be able to teach (Primary Schools Research and Development Group 1983). Does this mean that music was a low priority in primary school? Hardly. Many primary schools[3] went to the trouble of arranging for musicians working in the community to carry out projects in their school (DES 1978; DES 1982; DES 1985). Others appointed special music teachers. Long before the National Curriculum[4] was introduced, so that no school was obliged to teach music, advertisements for primary posts referred to music more frequently than any other subject. However, the special music teachers tended to operate in different ways from teachers with curriculum responsibility in any other subject. Whereas mathematics curriculum leaders, for instance, often operated mainly as coordinators of the school mathematics curriculum, and as advisers to their colleagues, music curriculum leaders were more likely to take over the music of several classes, whilst their own teachers were busy elsewhere. In other words, music curriculum leaders tended to operate as specialists, not as consultants.

This remains the case today. Moreover, in recent years, more primary schools have received projects given by musicians working in the community, or from arts organizations such as orchestras. While many of these projects are

---

[1] In the Primary Survey (DES 1978: 21), HMI found that 40 per cent of 7-year-olds, 50 per cent of 9-year-olds, and 55 per cent of 11-year-olds were taught music by someone other than their class teacher. There was no other subject in which fewer pupils were taught by their class teacher.

[2] In a survey of the opinions of 465 primary teachers, the Primary Schools Research and Development Group (1983) found that 26.6 per cent of teachers thought there was little need for all teachers to be able to teach music. A total of 19.6 per cent of teachers thought there was little need for all teachers to be competent in Religious Education. The percentages given for all other subjects were substantially lower.

[3] According to a series of HMI surveys (DES 1978, 1982, 1985), around 80 per cent of primary schools of at least moderate size had a teacher with special curriculum responsibility for music. No other subject had more teachers with special responsibility.

[4] Analysis of references to subjects in advertisements for initial primary posts in the *Times Educational Supplement* over various periods during the 1980s consistently showed more mention of music than any other subject. Interestingly, music remained the most sought-after subject strength in an analysis that I carried out over a three-week period in the spring of 1989, a time when one might have expected primary schools to be attempting to develop their subject strengths in mathematics, English, and science, in anticipation of the introduction of the National Curriculum in these subjects in September 1989.

excellent, and promote pupils' learning and enthusiasm, others are not. It is easy for school teachers to be dazzled by the musical skills of visiting musicians. It is worth bearing in mind that many visiting musicians are not qualified teachers, and that they may have less understanding than school teachers about how pupils learn, what they can achieve, and the expectations that the government makes of schools.

The idea of generalist music teaching is not a new one. The Plowden Report (CACE 1967) came out in favour of it more than 40 years ago. So why is music still so often taught by teachers who only, or mainly, teach that subject? There are, I think, two main, linked, reasons. First, many class teachers lack confidence in their ability to teach music. Second, many music curriculum leaders have not developed an ability to raise the confidence of their colleagues. In other words, these curriculum leaders have not learnt to act as consultants to generalists without specialist music skills. The same is true of some of the community musicians who visit primary schools with the aim of supporting the teaching there.

Most primary teachers received their own primary music teaching at the hands of music specialists who displayed formal skills such as piano playing and conducting. Today's music specialists are also able to draw on these skills when they wish to help pupils achieve a musical objective. There are, as we shall see, hardly any situations in which display of these skills is crucial to pupils' progress; teachers usually have a number of options concerning their teaching style. Specialists use specialist skills out of habit or preference, not necessity. But because they often appear to use these skills as a matter of course, their performance can seem intimidating and unachievable to outsiders. Primary music can seem to be about the demonstration of teacher skills, not the promotion of pupils' learning.

Generalists often arrive at their professional training with a well-established low confidence in their ability to teach music. When I began to work with generalists in training, in the 1980s, I found that music was the subject which worried them most initially (Mills 1989b), and the time that is available for music in initial training courses has roughly halved since then. Many primary trainees attribute their low confidence to an inability to emulate the teaching style of the music teachers they remembered from their own primary education. They speak of what they perceive to be their own musical inadequacies; perhaps they do not play the piano, or perhaps they are not confident singers. Often, sadly, they first decided that they were inadequate as musicians when a primary teacher criticized their musicianship. The story most frequently told was one of rejection from a primary-school choir.

These aspiring teachers measured their musical competence by what they could not do. Measurement of what they *can* do would be more to the point.

Every aspiring teacher I have met is able to do a great deal. Nearly all enjoy listening to some particular styles of music. Many have experience of playing one or more instruments, perhaps by ear. These are musical activities which can be shared with school pupils, and from which new skills and interests grow. But teachers and trainees bring much more than their music skills to their music teaching: they bring their teaching expertise. The teaching skills that teachers use to facilitate pupils' learning in mathematics, English, and so on, can be applied to music too. Music teaching is not about teachers performing to pupils; it is about children learning. Performing to pupils is only one way of helping pupils to learn. There are many situations in which other teaching techniques are equally, if not more, effective.

Although many aspiring primary teachers lack confidence in music, others have no such worries. Perhaps they have taken piano lessons for some years, or achieved an A level[5] in music. They may have taken some optional extra courses in music while they were studying as teachers, or they may have entered a teacher training course on completion of a music degree. Such student teachers have a head start over their colleagues. This is not just because they have skills which the others lack; there are ways of getting round that. Their advantage is that they already have musical self-esteem. They can make positive statements about their abilities and achievements as composers, performers, and listeners. They may feel that the pattern of their musical development has been uneven. Perhaps they have specialized in performing at the expense of composing, or perhaps their listening experience has been narrow. But they know that they start music teaching from a position of some strength.

We seek to develop musical self-esteem in those whom we teach. We want them to feel satisfaction when they achieve something worthwhile. The view that pupils with self-esteem achieve more, and that the relationship is, to some extent, causal, underpins much contemporary educational practice. Pupils are agreed to generally accomplish more when encouraged to think positively about their strengths and achievements, whilst remaining sensitive to the possibility of further development. Failure motivates but rarely. The politicians who used to think otherwise[6] have generally adjusted their views.

If self-esteem is good for pupils, then it seems likely that it is good for teachers teaching music. Teachers with musical self-esteem can enable less confident colleagues to develop it. First, they can tackle the matter head on.

---

[5] A levels, Advanced Level General Certificates of Education, still exist as academic examinations routinely taken by 18-year-olds.

[6] For example, in 1987 Oliver Letwin MP wrote that pupils 'had better learn from the earliest possible age to come to terms with their own capabilities' (Letwin 1987).

They can encourage colleagues to list their skills, and help them to develop approaches to music teaching that they feel ready to try. Second, they can show, through at least occasional demonstration of teaching approaches, within the reach of generalist colleagues, that it is possible to teach music without recourse to special skills. This means thinking about the options that teachers have when deciding how to help pupils to achieve a musical objective, and not always making a 'specialist' selection.

Teachers under stress can revert to teaching as they were taught, whatever the content and approach of their teacher training. As most teachers are the product of a specialist system of primary music teaching, this is an obstacle to the development of generalist music teaching. Faced with a colleague who is worried about teaching music, a music curriculum leader may be tempted to teach the class personally, rather than help the other's development in music teaching. This does not promote the development of the generalist's self-esteem. Nor does it develop musical self-esteem in the pupils involved, for they become aware that music cannot be handled by everyone. Through musical consultancy, rather than specialist music teaching, a more positive cycle of musical confidence can be generated. Pupils become the teachers of tomorrow. The musical self-esteem of teachers will, progressively, rise.

Music is, as we have seen, a subject of extremes. It has most specialist teachers, is taught by fewest class teachers, and is the subject in which most trainee teachers feel least confident. But it is far from a doomed subject. What we need to do is to channel the abilities of all those specialists away from perpetuating the myth that primary music can be taught only by those like them, and towards the development of more generalist music teaching.

Towards music teaching

Up to now we have concentrated on the importance of all teachers learning to lead musical activities with pupils. But activities alone do not make a curriculum. We need to think also about the aims and purposes of music teaching, and about balance, progression, and evaluation. We must consider the relationship of music to the whole primary curriculum, and the role of music within the life of the school. In other words, we need some sort of theoretical framework for our teaching. I take the view that the idea of a framework makes more sense when teachers already have experience of leading musical activity. The structure of this book reflects this view. The development of a theoretical framework is left to Part II. In Part I, the focus is on the organization of music-making. Aims, planning and preparation, evaluation, progression, links with other subjects, and so on, are addressed only on a day-to-day level. The context of this music-making is simply a music curriculum which is active, for all, and fun. There is an emphasis on the variety of approaches which teachers of differing taste and experience may use to involve pupils in music-making. Part I is, in a sense, teacher-centred.

Part II is more pupil-centred. Following a chapter on aspects of pupils' development in music, the subject of curriculum planning is addressed. Music is then set within the primary curriculum and, finally, within the primary school. No single framework for primary music could suit all schools or teachers. Much depends on the participating pupils and teachers, the school ethos, prevailing local and national government policies, and so on. Consequently, I do not provide any blueprints. The information here is intended to help teachers develop their own framework, and to design and implement a curriculum that fits their particular circumstances.

The whole of this book is addressed to all teachers, and all other musicians working in school. There is no special section for generalists, or one for music consultants, or one for visiting musicians. Initially, the needs of generalists and consultants, in particular, may differ in emphasis. Generalists starting to teach music may at first be preoccupied with finding activities with which they can cope. Other readers may be concerned more with developing their range of teaching approaches, with curriculum development, or with other long-term issues. But even the most hesitant generalists soon become able to take significant personal responsibility for their music teaching. The relationship between generalists and consultants in music stabilizes to become no different from that in other subjects. Both generalists and consultants become involved in the development and implementation of school music policy. So all teachers will, eventually, want to think about the matters dealt with in Part II.

Whenever possible, I avoid the use of musical jargon. Where inclusion of a term which may be unfamiliar to some readers seems unavoidable, its first appearance is accompanied by a few words of explanation. Staff notation—sometimes called stave notation or conventional music notation—does not appear at all. Many teachers can read music, or are learning to do so. But a book that contains staff notation is impenetrable to those who cannot already read it fluently. Since much primary music—possibly all—can be taught effectively without recourse to staff notation, there is no point in including it here. Teachers who do read music will have no difficulty in seeing how to apply this skill to their teaching, when they feel that this is appropriate.

Writing a book which is accessible to all teachers has involved careful choice of language, but no compromise of musical or educational purpose. There is nothing second-best about a properly organized and supported system of generalist music teaching.

STARTING POINTS FOR MUSICAL ACTIVITY

Music consists of the interrelated activities of composing, performing, and listening. The interrelation has two main facets. First, it is difficult to think of anything in music that does not involve at least two of these activities. Composers try out bits of their developing compositions by playing them, and listening to how they sound. Performers experiment with different ways of playing other people's compositions, and judge these by their sound. Members of the audience at even the most sedate of classical concerts can be seen tapping their feet, and showing their appreciation (or occasionally lack of appreciation) of a performance through applause. In some forms of music-making, for example much jazz, it makes no sense to try to differentiate between composers and performers, because everyone is both of these. Second, the three activities have a common factor: they are all creative. Creativity is not just an attribute of composers. Performers are not automatons, concerned exclusively with accuracy; their interpretation of a composition reflects their personal style. Listeners are not just pieces of blotting paper; they have differing personal responses to the same performance.

But despite the interrelation, we can think of music as a sequential creative process:

composing → performing → listening

which can be entered at any of three stages. At the first stage of this process we have composers who devise music. They may also, simultaneously, perform and listen. At the second stage we have performers who interpret music which is already composed. They may also be listening. At the third stage we find listeners who listen to the performance of others. They are not, at that moment, either composing or performing. In general, I have organized the musical activities in Part I according to where pupils are entering this sequence. Activities in which pupils devise music are found in Chapter 3, 'Composing'. This is followed by Chapter 4, 'Performing', which focuses on the interpretation of music that has already been composed. Finally, Chapter 5, 'Listening', deals with activities in which pupils enter the sequence as members of an audience.

In each chapter I draw attention to a range of possible approaches to teaching music. Teachers new to music can start with approaches that they find comfortable, although they should be aware that they are making a choice, that others might choose differently, and that they may wish to choose differently themselves on a later occasion. More experienced music teachers may wish to explore less familiar approaches in a more systematic way.

But before getting involved in composing, performing, and listening per se, we take a look in Chapter 2 at an educationally valuable form of music-making which can include any, or all, of the three activities, and which can serve as an effective introduction to class music for teachers: music games.

Chapter 2

Music games

The dread of beatings! Dread of being late!
And, greatest dread of all, the dread of games!

John Betjeman, in *Summoned by Bells*, VII:
'Marlborough' (Betjeman 1960: 67)

John Betjeman was not referring to music games. There is, so far as I am aware, nothing dreadful about music games. Quite the contrary. Pupils find them fun, and so do teachers, even those who are very worried about teaching music. In music games, there is often little need for the teacher to do anything musical at all. In some games, the teacher needs only to explain the game, tell the pupils when to start, and observe them whilst the game takes its natural course. In others, the teacher will be involved as a musician, but will be able to set himself or herself musical tasks substantially easier than those being presented to the pupils. In any case, the structure of the game is used to manage the development of the activity. Inexperienced teachers do not then find their carefully organized lesson plans disintegrating around them as a pupil responds to a task in a seemingly inexplicable manner. The teacher and pupils have met together to play a game, and that is what they do.

Music games must, of course, have some musical purpose. This means that they must involve pupils in at least one of the three processes of listening, performing, composing. And if they are to form a useful part of a progressive music education, games must enable us to observe something about the pupils' abilities or needs as composers, performers, or listeners, so that we can think about what to offer them next. This means that there are two musical questions to be asked about the games we consider:

1. What composing, listening, or performing are the pupils doing? (Musical process)

2. What can the teacher learn about the pupils' musicianship? (Musical assessment)

And because primary teachers teach pupils for the whole curriculum, not just music, there is a third question:

3. What else can the teacher learn about the pupils? (General assessment)

We shall return to these questions when we consider activities other than games.

The games here are described in more detail than most of the other activities. This is because many readers of this chapter may be inexperienced in music teaching, though experienced in teaching other areas of the primary curriculum. I want to illustrate some points that underpin music and music teaching. These include the following:

1. **Music cannot be rushed.**
   Time is one of the raw materials of music. You cannot listen to, or perform, a piece on 'fast forward'.

2. **Pattern in music cannot be perceived unless it is sustained.**
   This point is linked to the previous one. It takes time, and repetition, for a pattern to be recognized as such. Recognizing pattern helps us to make sense of music.

3. **Though hearing is the dominant sense in music, the other senses are important too.**
   Sight and sound often act together in the coordination of music, for example in conducting. Touch, and memory of touch, are crucial to some forms of performing. Any sensory experience may act as a stimulus for composition.

4. **Making mistakes, and recovering from them, is a crucial component of performing.**
   Even the most accomplished performers make mistakes. Pupils need to learn to recover from their mistakes, and those of others: a performance need not be stopped whenever something goes wrong.

5. **Group music-making is shared.**
   Performers support and help each other; they are not in competition.

6. **Extraneous sound can detract from music.**
   Music is a function of sound in time. Competing sound, such as that of the teacher's voice, can interfere with musical perception and appreciation.

7. **Music comes in a variety of styles.**
   In particular, music need have neither a recognizable melody, nor a regularly repeating pulse.

Music games can be used in many ways. As warm-up activities, they can capture pupils' interest, and focus their attention at the start of a substantial music lesson. As fill-in activities, they can act as freestanding mini music lessons. Some can eliminate the tedium from repetitive learning. As cooperative activities, they can promote the development of bonding within a class, and between a class and their teacher. But here we consider the games as activities in their own right.

Music games come in a variety of forms. Three types are included here:

◆ Classroom music games
◆ Traditional music games
◆ Music games with borrowed structures

Readers may find it helpful to try out some games with pupils before moving on to subsequent chapters.

Classroom music games

These are music games that have been devised specifically for classroom use. Two contrasting games are described here: Switch and Conductor. Both of these games, in various versions, have been frequently played in classrooms, and both can be found in other books.[1] The version of Switch suggested here is an adaptation of the published version.

Switch

Switch is suitable for full classes, or smaller groups. It is a structured copying game enjoyed by pupils of any primary age, but it is described here with older primary pupils in mind. Though some pupils become confident enough to lead Switch, it is perhaps best if the teacher first introduces it. Sit with the pupils in a circle and explain the game like this: 'I am going to perform some patterns. Join in with me. When I change patterns, you change too.' Without saying anything else, start clapping your hands regularly, at a comfortable pace (perhaps two claps a second). Once the pupils have all joined in, move to another simple pattern–perhaps slapping your knees at the same pace. When the pupils change from clapping to slapping, you know that they have understood the game, and are ready to try some more patterns. Stay on each pattern long enough for pupils to feel the repetition in what they are doing—at least fifteen seconds for easy patterns, and longer for more complicated ones—and move continuously between patterns so that the beat is maintained and the whole game becomes a continuous piece of music. Try to choose patterns that all pupils can join in with accurately after a few tries, but if you happen to choose a pattern which one or more pupils cannot manage, do not persist

---

[1] Switch is in *Pompaleerie Jig* (Thompson and Baxter 1978) and Conductor is in *Sounds Fun* (Wishart 1975).

with it, but move to another, easier, pattern to get the group back together again. In an introductory game of Switch, it is probably best to include a sequence of at least eight patterns drawn from the following categories:

Simple regular patterns at the same pace as the introductory clapping
Instead of clapping, stamp one or both feet, for instance.

Complex regular patterns, still at the same pace
Instead of clapping repeatedly, try **clap-clap-slap-clap, clap-clap-slap-clap** or **clap-clap-click, clap-clap-click**. (I have never learned to click my fingers, but this is not a problem. Pupils realize what I am trying to do, copy my gesture, and supply a click as well. However, I understand that teachers who *can* click occasionally meet pupils who are upset because they *cannot*! One teacher resolved this by supplying a mouth click simultaneously with the finger click. Perhaps there are advantages in being a non-clicking teacher . . .)

Simple regular patterns at half or a quarter of the pace of the introductory clapping
Try standing up for a count of four claps and then sitting down for another four, or placing your hands on the floor for a count of two claps, then on your lap for another two.

Irregular patterns
You might clap the rhythm of 'Polly put the kettle on', or 'We'll all have tea' from the end of the same nursery rhyme. If the pupils find that easy, try replacing the clap for 'tea' with a slap.

It is best not to spoil the impression of Switch as a continuous piece of music by giving the pupils any verbal instructions once it has started. End the game by folding your arms, or resting your hands on your lap. The pupils copy, and the game finishes.

What is the musical purpose of Switch? Let us refer back to the three questions at the beginning of this chapter:

1. What composing, listening, or performing are the pupils doing? (Musical process)

2. What can the teacher learn about the pupils' musicianship? (Musical assessment)

3. What else can the teacher learn about the pupils? (General assessment)

In Switch, the pupils' main role is as performers. They are taking part in a piece of music composed by the leader. They perform by recognizing, and repeating, patterns in the composition. They learn patterns that they could reuse in other music-making. Repeating of patterns helps pupils to learn how to anticipate sounds, and the movements that cause them: an important aspect of performance. In the spirit of the game, the pupils make an effort to recognize each pattern as soon as possible—thus increasing their skill in pattern recognition. As they repeat patterns, they develop their physical coordination, so are likely to be able to perform even better in the future. As well as performing, the pupils are listening. Sight is important in this game too, and many pupils rely on *seeing* the pattern. During Switch, teachers can become aware of the differing abilities of pupils in these physical skills. The gross body movement involved makes it relatively easy to spot pupils with difficulties in pattern recognition or physical coordination. Pattern recognition underpins learning in other subjects too. A pupil who seems to lack it in Switch merits investigation of pattern recognition in mathematics and art, for instance.

Is Switch just a one-off activity, or is there some value in playing it on several occasions? Of course pupils will become bored if they are forever playing Switch—particularly if the patterns are too easy, or impossible. But Switch can be developed in a number of ways to musical purpose. Here are three suggestions.

1. **Making Switch more difficult**
   Switch would be more challenging if one spent less time on each pattern. But this would be at the expense of some of the musical value of the game, for pupils would no longer have the musical experience of participating in repeating rhythmic patterns. Instead, try clapping some more challenging patterns, such as a line from *Ring a Ring o' Roses* or *Humpty Dumpty Sat on a Wall*. Next, you could use mixed body sounds to convey these rhythms, or you might prefer to make up some patterns of the length you want. The patterns can be as complicated as you like, provided that you can sustain them and the pupils can copy them.

2. **Asking a pupil to lead Switch**
   Some pupils respond well to the responsibility of leading Switch. The leader, of course, becomes the composer as well as a performer. If you have led Switch a few times with the group, leaders will probably understand that you expect them to produce patterns which others can copy, and that each pattern should be sustained for some time. But just occasionally you may need to intervene when a pupil leads with the intention of catching people out. Usually, your main role will be supportive; attentive copying by you helps leaders to clarify and remember their patterns. Having a pupil lead Switch is of value to all the pupils present—not just to the one who is leading. It helps to dispel any notion that music is something that teachers lead and pupils follow.

A group of 10-year-olds follow their teacher in a game of Switch. Note the extent to which they are seeing the pattern.

3. **Changing the rules**

   Try playing Switch Two. This starts like Switch, with the leader repeating a pattern and the pupils copying. After a while, you move on to pattern two, but the pupils stay on pattern one. When you say 'Switch', the pupils move to pattern two. After the pupils have repeated pattern two for a while, you move to pattern three, with the pupils joining you after you say 'Switch', and so on. Pupils are likely to find Switch Two much harder than Switch. Start by choosing very easy patterns such as repeated, even clapping, or repeated, even slapping, until the pupils have mastered the idea of the overlap. In Switch Two, pupils learn to recognize a new pattern whilst sustaining an old one, and become less dependent on the leader. Thus they are developing their performing skills, increasing their own responsibility for the accuracy of their performance, and, probably, becoming more observant of the performance of other pupils.

Conductor

Like Switch, Conductor can be played by full classes, or smaller groups. Again, it is suitable for a wide age range, though young pupils are probably best introduced to it in a small group. As in Switch, it is best to introduce

Conductor by leading it yourself. Sit the pupils in a circle, and stand in the centre. Ask each pupil to think of a sound she or he can make, and then hear them one at a time, making suggestions to anyone who has not thought of a sound (e.g. 'Clap, or say "Ah" '). Once a sound has been heard, each pupil is expected to stick to his or her own sound until a new leader is chosen. Next, explain the game like this: 'I am a conductor, and you are my orchestra. When I point to you, start making your sound. Carry on, until I show you that I want you to stop.' After checking that the pupils understand your signs for starting and stopping, compose a piece by directing pupils to start and stop playing as you wish. Again, do not issue any verbal instructions. If you want a pupil to play louder, softer, or differently, you must show them with an appropriate signal. Pupils then take it in turns to conduct the orchestra.

Again, we will evaluate this activity by considering the musical process, and the opportunities for musical assessment and general assessment (see pp. 11–12).

In Conductor, as in Switch, the leader is composing, the group is performing, and everybody, one hopes, is listening. But the nature of the composing and performing that are taking place is different. Switch always results in a piece based on short repeating patterns. Conductor can result in pieces with no observable rhythmic structure.[2] Switch results in a composition that is linear or—in the case of Switch Two—has two overlapping strands. In Conductor, pieces can have as many layers as there are pupils. From observing pupils whilst they are members of the orchestra, a teacher can see their level of concentration, and ability to control their performance according to the conductor's instructions. Watching pupils conduct gives insights into their development as composers.

I once played Conductor with a class of 9-year-olds whom I had not met previously. We were using percussion instruments, not body sounds. After leading the game myself once, I asked for volunteers. I was not impressed by the compositions produced by the first three conductors. They were high-spirited boys who enjoyed the power of leading the game, but did not seem to spend much time listening to the results of their instructions. They were acting as though they were on point duty, rather than being in charge of an orchestra. Their compositions consisted of a succession of very loud sections

---

[2] I do not mind if a piece I am conducting ends up with no discernible pulse. Such a piece is sometimes described as a soundscape. But leaders who, at least initially, do not feel comfortable with this sort of piece can often engineer a pulse by choosing as their first performer a child who produces a regular, and loud, sound. Performers who enter later will usually fit in with this pulse.

which were so short that we never had a chance to get used to them before they changed. These pupils were not used to being given this sort of responsibility and they were acting as though they might never be given it again. When a fourth boy volunteered, I noticed some of the other pupils nudging each other. Robert was an immature pupil who could hardly read or write. The other pupils seemed to think that he would be a hopeless leader. Nothing could have been further from the truth. With great assurance, Robert pointed to a triangle, and listened to it being played for a full ten seconds before directing the player to stop. He turned to a tambourine and listened to it for a similar length of time before directing that player, also, to stop. He turned to the triangle again, and when it had played for a few seconds, brought the tambourine in on top of it. He listened to the two sounds together for a while, and directed the tambourine to play a little louder to achieve the balance he wanted. His piece continued with the same care. Robert used silence as well as sound. Finally, after three or four minutes, Robert brought his piece to a gentle, but purposeful, conclusion. When he sat down, there was a short silence, and then the pupils, quite spontaneously, applauded. Robert had shown us all a lot about his musicianship. He had also made everyone present start to listen closely to the sounds they, and everyone else, were producing. He had earned the respect of his peers, and done wonders for his own self-esteem.

   Neither Switch nor Conductor requires teachers to have musical skills more advanced than those of the pupils they are leading. Indeed, leading Switch, and certainly Switch Two, is easier than playing it. The teacher manages the activities through teaching skill, not musical skill.

Traditional games

Many adults recall playing singing games and clapping games as pupils. *London Bridge is Falling Down* and a clapping game, *A Sailor Went to Sea*, are two that I remember from my own primary-school playground in Manchester. In former times, singing games were a diversion for adults as well as pupils. Today, they have moved firmly into pupil culture. Pupils, mainly girls, organize them for themselves in some school playgrounds. And adults lead some with young girls and boys at home, in playgrounds, and in the earliest stages of the primary school. Can these games form part of primary music? Let us consider one in particular: *Ring a Ring o' Roses*.

Ring a Ring o' Roses

This singing game is found in a multitude of versions. However, it is generally agreed that this is the first verse:

> Ring a ring o' roses,
> A pocket full of posies.
> A-tishoo! A-tishoo!
> We all fall down.

Usually, everyone skips in a ring until the end of the verse, when they fall on the floor.

This is an old singing game, although quite how old is not known. The original meaning of the words is uncertain. One story—which is probably not true—is that the game dates from the Great Plague of 1665, with the four lines of the verse denoting, respectively, the plague rash, herbs carried as protection against infection, the sneezes of the dying, and their demise. Iona and Peter Opie (Opie and Opie 1985), who collected and researched pupils' traditional games over many years, attribute the supposed association, perhaps a little cynically, to 'satisfaction of the adult requirement that anything seemingly innocent should have a hidden meaning of exceptional unpleasantness'. They found no reference to the game being played in England earlier than the mid-nineteenth century.

Suppose that a small group of 5-year-olds are playing *Ring a Ring o' Roses*, led by their teacher. In what musical processes are the pupils participating? And what can the teacher learn from their response? This is a performing and listening game. The pupils are singing a song, and combining it with some physical actions which may be in time with the music. They may not sing the song perfectly in tune, but are having the sort of practice which does, with most pupils, result in them progressively learning to sing better in tune. They are listening, because they sing the song at roughly the same pace as everyone else. As in Switch, they may also be guided by looking, particularly at the moment when they should fall down.

The teacher learns about the pupils' singing ability and their rhythmic awareness. Some pupils may always sing below the pitch that she chooses but move up and down at roughly the correct points. Others may use a very limited range of notes, or even only one note. A few may not have found their singing voice: they may be speaking. This is information that the teacher can use to help pupils develop their singing in the future. Some pupils may be anticipating the moment when they fall down, thus demonstrating that they know the song, and are able to think ahead.

The range of traditional singing games and clapping games is considerable. In *The Singing Game*, Iona and Peter Opie listed over 150 such games, many of which come in several versions. Some, such as *Ring a Ring o' Roses, Oranges and Lemons*, and *London Bridge is Falling Down*, are well known in many areas of the UK, and appear in many pupils' songbooks. But singing games are being invented, changed, introduced into contemporary teaching materials, and brought into the country by pupils all the time. Teachers can learn a lot about pupils from just watching them playing games in the playground. And that is surely not musically threatening to anyone.

As well as traditional singing and clapping games, there are some other well-known music games which are sometimes played at pupils' parties. Musical Chairs and Musical Statues are two examples. Pupils move round while music plays. When it stops, they either race to sit on a chair (of which there are too few available) or become still as a statue, as appropriate. These are competitive games usually played when there is an adult available to adjudicate on matters such as who got to the chair first, or whether Chloë moved or not. Too much competition in school music is not a good thing. But these games are not completely devoid of musical value. They may help pupils to learn to move in time to music, for once one pupil does this, others often copy. And pupils have to listen, not just treat the music as background. Otherwise they will soon be 'out'.

Music games with borrowed structures

Most games can, with a little imagination, be turned into music games. Take Hunt the Thimble, for instance. Instead of saying 'getting warmer' or 'getting colder', as a pupil hunts the thimble that was hidden whilst she was out of the room, pupils can be asked to sing a note which gets louder as the hunter gets closer. This challenges the hunter as a listener, and the rest as performers; it is not easy to control the loudness of sung notes, particularly long notes. There are many possible variations of this game. Sung notes could get higher as the hunter approaches the thimble. Or clapping could get faster, for instance.

Bingo can be played using instrument sounds instead of numbers. The bingo cards might show pictures of the instruments, which would be played out of view. During Musical Snakes and Ladders, for instance, there could be special sounds for going up ladders and down snakes, and, perhaps, some musical tasks to perform if particular squares are landed on. Figure 1 shows a composing board game which I have called Coach Trip. As in an ordinary board game, the object is to get from the start to the finish using a sequence of dice throws. In this case, the game re-creates a recent school trip from Oxford to Stratford. Whilst dice throwing is taking place, the players sing songs they sang on the coach. When a counter lands on a square with instructions, the players, as a group, compose a suitable piece.[3] The teacher is free to invent his

---

[3] Determining the details of the music we compose by the throw of a die is not as unmusical as it might at first seem. Some twentieth-century composers have employed chance procedures in their compositions. For example, some of the material in John Cage's *Music of Changes* for piano (1951) was determined by the toss of a coin.

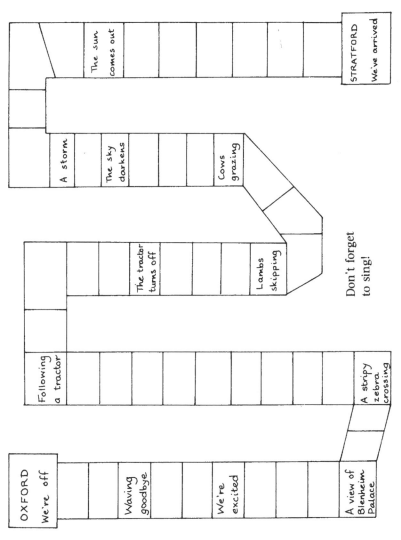

Fig. 1 Coach Trip, a board game for some Oxford children who had recently returned from a school trip to Stratford.

or her own rules about matters such as whether the final square must be reached by an exact throw, how the instructions for compositions should be interpreted, and whether there is one team, or rival teams. Board games may follow the line of a story, perhaps *Jack and the Beanstalk*. They may take pupils on real or fantastic journeys, or in quest of buried treasure. The possibilities are almost limitless.

But games are only one way of facilitating composition. In the next chapter we turn to some other approaches.

Chapter 3

Composing

The material of music is sound and silence. Integrating these is composing.

John Cage in *Silence* (Cage 1962: 150)

What is composing?

Composing is not just about producing string quartets that Mozart might have written if he had lived longer, or writing substantial orchestral works for first performance at the Henry Wood promenade concerts. Composing takes place whenever a person (or group of people) devises a piece of music. It may be a ten-day opera cycle based on *The Complete Works of Shakespeare*, a one-minute setting of a haiku, or a popular song. It may use the resources of a full symphony orchestra, or three chime bars.

I shall use the term 'composing' to encompass all acts of musical invention by anyone in any style, or blend of styles. Thus I take activities such as improvising or arranging to be particular styles of composing, not distinct processes.[1] I shall describe the people composing—be they adults or pupils, highly qualified or inexperienced—as composers, and the pieces of music they produce as compositions. In this, I am observing the conventions of other arts areas. We speak of pupils and adults as writing and being writers, whether their output, their writing, is an account of yesterday's visit to the zoo, a daily diary entry, or a novel shortlisted for the Man Booker Prize. We speak of pupils and adults as painters whether they paint their paintings in a classroom, at evening class, or in a garret.

Composing in school

Visit any primary school, and you are likely to observe pupils making art: painting, writing poems, and so on. But you may not observe anyone

---

[1] In improvising, the composing and performing take place at the same time; the performer composes as she or he goes along. Arranging consists of adapting another composition. Thus a composer might make a piano arrangement of a folk melody, or of a work by Handel.

Group composing. The boys here are working together, and not as individuals.

composing. Why is this? The simplest answer is that music in school traditionally has stressed performing and listening at the expense of composing. Primary
teachers rarely composed when they were at school. Those who studied music
after they left school trained, typically, as performers, not composers. This is
changing. The amount of composing going on in primary and secondary
schools has been increasing for some time. Many of the marks in GCSE and A
level music are allocated to composing. Many students entering initial teacher
training already accept composing as an integral part of music-making. But for
several decades to come there will still be primary teachers whose experience of
pupils composing is second-hand. These teachers can, quite understandably,
feel some uncertainty about how to approach composing with pupils.

Many opportunities for composing arise naturally as part of classroom
activity. A pupil who has written a poem may offer to make it into a song. A
group of pupils who have improvised a drama about a haunted house may
want to include music to set a spooky atmosphere. Here, the teacher's job is to
encourage the pupils—to facilitate their development of their own idea—and
to respond to their work when it is complete. But we cannot rely on pupils'
ideas alone for a programme of composing. We need to promote situations in
which pupils wish to compose, provide input to enrich their composing, and
respond to their work to help them learn from it.

I shall focus on approaches to composing that are collaborative, involving
pupils working together as a class or in smaller groups. I do this for two

Individual composing. Nadia has been composing alone on the glockenspiel, with great concentration, for more than half an hour.

reasons. First, group composition is easier to manage. It demands fewer resources, and requires the teacher to be in fewer places at once. A class of thirty pupils in small groups requires fewer reasonably quiet working spaces than the same number of individuals would need. Second, group composition offers more opportunity for learning. For most people, composing is not about sitting in front of a blank wad of music manuscript paper and waiting for the muse to provide inspiration, but a form of problem-solving. John Paynter (Salaman 1988: 29) speaks of his own composing as 'setting up problems for oneself, taking decisions that will answer those problems, and having the satisfaction of having answered them'. Composing in groups can enhance the processes of selection and rejection inherent in problem-solving. Group composing is not a hybrid procedure designed by music educators—a sort of educational composing. It takes place in the world outside school too. Much—though not all—jazz, for instance, is collaborative composition. However, pupils will of course sometimes prefer to compose on their own.

Getting started

How can a teacher introduce pupils to composing? Ideally, they introduce themselves to it. Young children are fascinated by sounds of all sorts: rustling paper and birdsong, as well as the sounds of singing and musical instruments.

Extensive opportunity to play with sounds can lead, without deliberate adult help, to the sequencing of a series of sounds to give a result that pleases the composer. This process is often seen, or rather heard, in children who make up songs from an early age.[2] And children who have a piano, or other instruments, in their homes often love to experiment on them. But many children arrive at school without this sort of experience.

From their earliest days in school, pupils can play with sound. This can be organized by means of a music corner, or a music table, in which pupils can play on their own, or in small groups. A music corner can contain many types of sound makers, not just official musical instruments. Pupils can be encouraged to bring interesting sounds to school, and to share them with other pupils. They can find a variety of sounds from the same sound maker, thus developing their association between physical action and the nature of sound. They can learn to listen closely to sounds, to talk about them, and compare them.

What about the noise? Certainly, there will be some. But teachers can learn to manage it. In the past, primary classrooms were often very quiet places, in which pupils spoke only to their teacher. Today, teachers tolerate a higher working noise level because they accept that pupils learn from talking to each other too. Like talk, music cannot take place in silence. And music tables are often distracting only whilst they are novel. Teachers who have introduced them often speak of ceasing to notice them by the end of a fortnight or so. This is not because the music table receives progressively less use, but because the teacher has learnt to regard the resulting sound as ambient noise. Particularly while music tables are being introduced, teachers can help themselves by including only fairly quiet sound makers. There is no need for the first instrument placed on the music table to be a large cymbal.

Pupils who grow up with music tables in their primary schools often start to compose of their own accord. Teachers can receive frequent requests to 'come and listen to what we've made up'. But one can sometimes meet an older class who have not been encouraged to play with sound in the past. In this situation, a more systematic approach to starting composing may be needed. A general instruction to the pupils to 'go and compose something' is unlikely to be productive; pupils who have not played with sound makers do not know what sounds are available to them, and cannot produce particular sounds consistently. Some initial familiarization with materials, and the sounds they produce, is necessary.

---

[2] An account of the development of song in pre-school children can be found in Hargreaves 1986.

A vast range of materials is available for composing: the voice and other body sounds, classroom percussion instruments, electronic resources of an ever increasing range and scope, the piano and orchestral instruments, recorders, improvised instruments, and so on. Initially, we will focus here on classroom percussion instruments. Most schools have at least a modest collection, and they are the first 'real' instruments that many pupils meet. Pupils of all ages can use them, often alongside other materials. And they can provide a way into music-making for musically deprived older pupils who are unlikely to be impressed by suggestions that they experiment with sounds produced by odds and ends, and who may be embarrassed at the thought of using their voices in an improvisatory way.

Materials 1: classroom percussion instruments

One sometimes hears, and reads, the statement that classroom instruments come in two categories: pitched and unpitched. This is misleading. The so-called unpitched instruments—woodblocks, cymbals, triangles, and so on—have sounds that include an element of pitch. Most people will agree that a triangle sounds higher than a woodblock, and that a small triangle sounds higher than a large one. Take a good-quality cymbal, and notice how the pitch of the sound changes as you hit it in different places, or with different beaters. The main way in which these instruments differ from the so-called pitched ones—glockenspiels, metallophones, xylophones,[3] chime bars, and so on—is that their pitches are not tuned to correspond to the notes found on the piano. It is more precise to speak of the two categories as tuned and untuned instruments.

Classroom instruments are expensive items. Many are also fragile. Matters concerning care, which seem obvious to us, can be less clear to young pupils. Many percussion instruments are played by being hit, an activity not often encouraged at school. If it is all right to hit some instruments, why not try hitting all of them? When we predict that we are likely to break a maraca if we hit it with the stick we have just used on a drum, we are drawing on many years of experience of hitting various objects and observing the results. When we hold a maraca (which should be part of a pair!), our experience of materials and their mass enables us to predict that the bulbous end is a thin, hollow, shell. Indeed, we may have seen a broken maraca, and so know that the shell is

---

[3] Xylophones have wooden bars, whereas metallophones and glockenspiels have metal ones. However, toy manufacturers, as opposed to musical instrument manufacturers, are not all clear about this. The fact that toy 'xylophones' sometimes have plastic or metal bars causes some children and teachers to become confused.

brittle. Similarly, when we predict that a triangle beater is likely to scratch, or even perforate, the head of a drum, we are drawing on experience of scratching which we would prefer pupils not to acquire on the school's expensive instruments.

Whatever care is taken, instruments will occasionally be broken. The size of the school music budget needs to reflect that limited life of instruments. And we cannot expect pupils to be creative with instruments if they are worried about breaking them. But pupils can learn to regard instruments as special, and to think before they act. Careful introduction of instruments helps with this, and also serves the musical purpose of encouraging pupils to observe closely, and learn to control, instrument sounds.

Instruments can be introduced one at a time, when the whole class is together. Try passing an instrument round the class, and encouraging experiment and talk. What different sounds does the instrument make? How can we describe the sounds? How is the instrument made, and how should we look after it? What is the instrument called? Are any of the sounds like those produced from other instruments? The following might form an extract from an introduction to a single maraca:

— How is Mayomi playing the maraca? . . .
— Yes, by flicking his wrist . . .
— How can you describe the sound he is making? . . .
— Mayomi, now play the maraca like Dean was doing, using more of your arm . . .
— How is the sound different?

Throughout the exercise, the emphasis is on listening, often very fine listening. Try not to give the impression that there is a single, official, way of playing any instrument, but encourage range and variety of sound, permitting any means of playing the instrument which cannot damage either it or the pupils. Once a range of sounds has been produced, several of the pupils have handled the instrument, and you are sure the points concerning care have been understood, the instrument can be placed on the music table, and pupils will do their own experimenting as the occasion arises. Later, you can share what the pupils have found. Gradually, other instruments could be introduced in a similar way. As new instruments are added to the music table, others may be removed temporarily. There is no need for pupils to have continual access to all instruments. Working with just a few resources from time to time can help to focus activity.

Why do I consider that official ways of playing instruments should not be stressed at this stage? I think that prescription of technique can constrain listening and thinking, and so impede musical development. I remember my introduction to the triangle, when I was about 6. My teacher said something like this:

> 'This is a triangle. See how I am holding it, so that the triangle hangs from the piece of string. Watch how I hit it . . . Now I'll hold the triangle while you hit it . . . Now try holding the triangle too.'

After a while, I did learn to hit the triangle without it twisting round on its string. But I cannot remember the sound it made—only the physical difficulty of producing it at the correct time. There was a sense in which the class percussion band became PE, not music, for me. And it was many years before I even thought of trying to find other ways of producing sounds from a triangle.

As I recall it, my first primary class included at least 50 pupils, and I am amazed that my teacher managed to give me any individual attention. I understand why, in this context, letting me experiment on a triangle before joining the percussion band would have seemed a pointless and noisy waste of time. But now, with more manageable class sizes, experiment is feasible. Of course there are times when I want a pupil to produce a neat 'ting-ting' from a triangle to give a particular effect. On these occasions I will, if necessary, direct the pupil to hold the instrument in a particular way. But, during composing, and many performing, activities, pupils can be left to choose the sound that they think is most effective. If they want the damped sound obtained when a triangle is held firmly in one hand, and hit close by, so be it.

So far I have focused on the effect of physical action on sound. If we perform a particular physical action, what sort of sound do we get? This is only one side of the relationship between sound and action. When we hear a sound, can we work out how it was made? Can we go to an instrument and repeat it? There are many ways of building up this association. Games can be useful. Two groups of pupils can be given equivalent sets of instruments and seated on either side of a screen. A member of one group plays a sound. The other group confer and then echo the sound. The teacher and the rest of the class are able to see both groups, and learn from finding out which sounds the pupils confuse. This is a taxing game; two or three contrasting instruments will be sufficient to begin with.

Materials 2: other resources

There are many other materials for composing. The instruments that pupils bring with them—their bodies—are a valuable resource. Vocal sounds, including singing, and other sounds such as clapping and stamping can add greatly to the range of sounds available. They need not be a last resort to be used when there are not enough percussion instruments, or there is no suitable ICT available; they

Alice is practising some of the less conventional piano sounds she has chosen to contribute to a class composition. She prefers to stand up so that she can see other members of her group, and reach the extremes of the keyboard with both hands.

are more suitable than other resources for some purposes. On p. 40 there is a report of a composition for which some pupils elected to use mainly vocal sounds, despite there being a large range of instruments available.

Pupils learning portable instruments, such as the violin or the recorder, can be invited to bring them to composing lessons. Composing strengthens the association between action and sound, and so also helps with performing. Instruments that belong to individual pupils are probably best played only by them because of the possibility of breakage. But a piano, if available, can be a useful resource for any pupil, not just those taking piano lessons. Like all instruments, it can be played in unconventional, as well as conventional, ways.

Recent developments in technology mean that computers and keyboards are now available in many primary classrooms. Often they can be integrated with

Steven and Gareth play electronic keyboards and amplify their vocal sounds, alongside David, who has chosen to play the bongos in this class composition.

other available materials. An increasing number of primary schools are obtaining musical software for computers. Some of it effectively converts the computer into a musical instrument which can be played alongside others. With other software, it is more appropriate for the pupils to compose using the computer alone.

Instruments can be improvised. Coconut shells are a permanent part of many instrument collections. Later, on p. 41, we shall see how items including vacuum cleaners may be used occasionally for particular effects. Pupils who find objects which make interesting sounds may wish to use them in composing activities.

Improvised instruments can be used to enrich the sounds available from a collection of classroom percussion instruments, but they cannot be substitutes. Given the cost of good classroom percussion instruments, it can be tempting to stock the percussion trolley with home-made ones. Unfortunately, many physically outlive their period of musical use. A yoghurt pot containing gravel does not sound as interesting as a pair of maracas. Once its maker has forgotten the excitement of assembling it, it is best disposed of. A yoghurt pot can be a very boring instrument to play. And when you become bored, you stop listening, and playing degenerates to become mere mechanical action.

Planning composing: the need for experiment

Pupils who have not played instruments for a while forget the sounds they make, and lose their control of them. Consequently, it is often expedient to start a composing lesson with an opportunity for experiment on the instruments available. Let us suppose that you have decided to take a full class composing lesson using classroom percussion instruments as your only sound materials. You have a class of 30 pupils, and 35 instruments available. How will you organize the experimentation?

You have a number of decisions to make. Will you allow the pupils to chose their own instrument? Will you offer them any guidance about their style of experimentation? How will you terminate the experiment? In general, I prefer to allow pupils to choose their own instrument, to permit them some unstructured experiment, and to end it through use of a prearranged signal, such as three taps on a drum.

Some teachers worry that pupils will start to behave badly if they are given percussion instruments. In fact, the high spirits which do sometimes arise are often the result of over-enthusiasm, rather than naughtiness. The pupils want to play the instruments, and they become impatient if a lot of time is spent on administration. This tendency towards over-enthusiasm is particularly strong amongst pupils who are rarely allowed to play instruments. In the words of an advisory teacher: 'If you are nine, and you have never played a drum before, and you think you might never play one again, you will give it a jolly good bash while you have the chance.' So when working with a new class, I always explain, right at the beginning, that:

◆ nobody is to play except when I say so
◆ this is so that we do not waste any of the time we could be using for playing.

Also, I waste as little time as possible by arranging the room so that instruments can be chosen and collected speedily. I find an arrangement in which the pupils are seated in a circle, and the instruments are on the floor in the middle, particularly efficient. You may have other ideas.

Once I have started the experiment with some statement such as 'see what different sounds you can produce from your instrument', I move among the pupils listening to what they are doing. When I decide that they have done enough experimenting—perhaps after a minute—I give the prearranged signal and everyone, usually, stops. There is no need to have a particularly loud signal. The point is that the pupils nearest you will stop immediately, and the rest soon follow them. After the experiment, I might ask some pupils to demonstrate their sounds, and make links into the composing we are going to do, if possible.

Sometimes, you will find a class surprisingly quiet during experiment. Later, you may wish to encourage them to find some loud sounds too. More often, classes will make plenty of noise. This is particularly likely if they have had infrequent access to instruments in the past. Problems of perpetual loud playing usually resolve themselves as pupils come to realize that they will meet the instruments again. You can accelerate this through musical ploys such as asking pupils to find quiet sounds as well as loud sounds. But it would be unmusical to ask pupils to 'experiment quietly'. Music is sometimes loud, and pupils need access to loud music as well as to quiet music, without feeling that they are being naughty.

A composing lesson

Composing often takes place as a small-group activity. But what might a composing lesson for a full class look like? Clearly, it could take many forms. Here is a single example of an initial lesson that I taught to a class of 8-year-olds. I got through the lesson, and the pupils appeared to appreciate it. But I feel, with hindsight, that 8-year-olds are actually capable of more than this. By the time that pupils in England are 8, they have been studying composing, as part of the National Curriculum, for three years, and many of them have been composing informally since their early childhood. There are other ideas for composing lessons suitable for primary-school children elsewhere in this book, and there are further ideas in books such as John Paynter's *Sound and Silence* (Paynter and Aston 1970) and *Sound and Structure* (Paynter 1992) which have sometimes mistakenly been thought to relate only to secondary-school students.[4] The lesson here is written up in such a way as to bring out some points that I want to make about planning, implementing, and evaluating composing activities. However, teachers and schools find their own ways of recording teaching, and the format I use here is intended as an example only, and not as a model.

---

[4] See also Glover and Young 1999; Young and Glover 1998.

Lesson plan: introduction to composing

GROUP	Class of 29 pupils aged 8/9
DURATION	Approximately 40 minutes
LOCATION	School hall

AIMS
(for lesson)

- To remind the pupils of group composing
- To reinforce the pupils' understanding of the concept of duration (long/short) in musical sound
- To introduce the pupils to symbolic notation

OBJECTIVES
(for pupils)

- To listen closely to the sounds that classroom instruments produce
- To find ways of producing sounds from instruments, particularly sounds of differing duration
- To use symbols to differentiate short sounds from long sounds
- To compose pieces that draw on resources of short and long sounds, and to notate these compositions symbolically
- To evaluate these compositions

MATERIALS   About 40 classroom percussion instruments. Paper and coloured pens

METHOD

1. Pupils choose instruments. Demonstrate the signal for stopping playing (clapping hands four times).

2. Pupils experiment to find three different sounds from their instruments. Listen to some of the sounds. Draw out the idea that some sounds are longer than others.

3. Pupils experiment to find the longest and shortest sounds that their instrument can produce. Listen to some pairs of sounds. How might sounds on particular instruments be made even longer or shorter? Are there some instruments that can make only fine differences between long and short? Listen carefully to a very long sound produced by a sustaining instrument, e.g. finger cymbals. Do we all think that it has died away at the same time?

4. Show my notation for a long sound followed by a short sound (see Fig. 2a). Can the pupils work out what it represents? Ask them to play it as a class. When I tell them to start, I want them to play their longest sound.

When that has finished, they are to play their shortest sound. The piece ends when the last short sound has finished.

5. Ask for suggestions for a slightly longer piece. Play it according to the same rules as Fig. 2a.

6. Ask for suggestions about a different way of playing the new piece. If there are no ideas, suggest that we synchronize the start of each sound by having a pupil playing a sustaining instrument directing us. Record us playing the piece that way, and play the recording back to the pupils. What do they think of it? How might we improve it? Or if everyone thinks it is wonderful, why do we like it so much?

7. Divide the class into five friendship groups, and give each group a sheet of paper and pen. Ask each group to make up a piece using the ideas of long and short. Each group should notate its composition. They can use the system of notation provided, or invent their own. Disperse the groups around the room. Check that groups are working profitably, but avoid the temptation to give them ideas unless they are stuck.

8. After about ten minutes, or earlier if everyone has finished, give the signal for pupils to stop playing. Ask each group to perform their piece and show their notation. Ask for comments from the composers and the audience on the pieces and the notation.

9. Discuss ways of taking these suggestions into account in future compositions.

REPORT (the numbers here correspond to the numbering of the method)

1. The pupils were excited by the prospect of playing the instruments, but showed commendable self-control. The signal worked well. The pupils nearest me stopped immediately, and everyone stopped within five seconds.

2. The pupils enjoyed doing this. I chose some examples of pupils playing conventionally, and less conventionally, for us to listen to, and tried not to give the impression that I was valuing some techniques more than others. The concept of long/short arose naturally from talking about two sounds which Pyashi had produced with the finger cymbals: tapping one with the other to produce a long sound, and bringing them together to produce a short sound.

3. The pupils quickly spotted that they had very little control over the duration of some instruments, for example, maracas. Robert's long maraca sound involved a longer arm movement, but very little difference in duration. We listened to the sounds with our eyes shut to confirm this.

While we were listening to Pyashi's long finger cymbal sound, some pupils furthest away from her noticed the whir of the fluorescent light. We discussed how the sound is always there when the light is switched on, but that we only notice it when we are listening very carefully.

4. This was straightforward.

5. Tony suggested the notation given as Fig. 2b.

6. Tony suggested that we synchronize our sounds, and I asked Pyashi to lead us from the finger cymbals. When we listened to the recording, Alex said that it sounded boring because the recording equipment had failed to pick up the quiet sounds at the end of the long sound. Hannah suggested that a long sound be deemed complete after a count of ten.

7. I moved round the groups as they worked, but they had plenty of their own ideas.

8. All groups used my system of notation. Four groups wrote longer linear combinations of dots and dashes. Two groups synchronized their sounds, and the other two expected individual players to be guided by their own instrument. The fifth group wrote two independent parts: one for long instruments that sustained well, and the other for short instruments that did not. There were more sounds in the part for short instruments (see Fig. 2c). The first four groups were impressed by the fifth group's idea. Comments about the other compositions were polite and general, for example, 'It was good'. There were no analytical comments, and no composers said anything about their own piece.

Fig. 2 Three long/short compositions. The third (c) has a separate part for short instruments which do not sustain well.

9. We discussed how we might make a longer piece using long and short sounds. The general consensus was that it would be interesting to develop further the idea of separate parts for long and short instruments.

COMMENT

We came some way towards accomplishing all the objectives. However, the pupils' evaluation, both of their own and other pupils' composing, was limited. The most productive evaluation was of the recording. In future lessons, perhaps I should make more use of recording, but also encourage constructive criticism of our own, and each other's, work.

FUTURE WORK

Short term   In the next lesson, we will work on producing a longer piece using long and short sounds.

Long term   I do not want the pupils to get stuck in a long/short rut. We will try other sorts of stimuli, and other approaches to notation including, of course, not using it at all.

The general points about composing lessons that I wish to draw out of this account are as follows:

1. **Use of stimulus**
   The stimulus here was 'long and short'. I chose it as a musical concept well within the reach of most pupils aged 8 years. But stimuli do not need to be musical concepts, and they can be used in a variety of ways.

2. **Choice of materials**
   Classroom percussion instruments provide a variety of long and short sounds. But I would have welcomed any suggestion from the pupils that body sounds, or IT resources, be included.

3. **Response to composition**
   There was time for reflection, discussion, and criticism, though this was not a particularly successful feature of the lesson.

4. **Appropriate use of notation**
   I chose a form of notation that reinforced the long/short concept. There is no value in using notation for its own sake.

5. **Facilities**
   The lesson suited the available facilities: a hall in which several groups would be able to work without distracting each other.

The remainder of this chapter develops these points.

Stimulus

Stimuli for composing can take many forms, including poems, objects, pictures, stories, words, pieces of music, and musical concepts. They are used to give composers starting points for their ideas. An effective stimulus helps composers, particularly those working in groups, to spend less time deciding what to do, and more time deciding how to do it. Stimuli can be chosen by teachers or composers. Indeed, a composer may think of one spontaneously. For instance, a pupil who has written a poem may, without any suggestion from a teacher, wish to set it to music.

An intended stimulus can become a constraint. Teachers need to intervene if no worthwhile work is being generated. Equally, they will sometimes wish to allow pupils who have deviated from the stimulus, but who are working productively, to see their ideas through.

Some stimuli can be interpreted more divergently than others. There are some occasions when teachers wish to allow pupils considerable freedom. At other times, perhaps when teaching a musical concept, teachers may wish to define the parameters for the composing more closely. Thus, in the long term, teachers often use a combination of types and levels of stimuli.

Earlier, on p. 34, I gave an example of a lesson plan based on the stimulus of a musical concept. Below, I use accounts of composing activities to illustrate some ways in which other types of stimuli may be applied. They are only examples; you will have your own ideas.

Stimulus 1: a poem written by a teacher

A class of pupils aged 9 years were to build a composition based on the topic, 'The Sea'. Their teacher wrote the following poem to remind her class of some images associated with the sea.

The Sea

Waves lap gently on the seashore
Fishes dart
Black clouds bring a raging storm
Out peeps the sun and shines upon a rainbow
Waves lap gently on the seashore

Sally Crowther

The teacher organized this poem carefully. Each line is short, and easily remembered. The contrasting first four lines suggest different styles of music. Repetition of the first line as the last line implies repetition of the first musical idea, thus enabling pupils to realize that they can repeat parts of their music.

After reading and discussing the poem with the pupils, the teacher read it one line at a time, inviting the pupils to improvise suitable music at the end of each line. Individuals produced different effects for each line. Lee, for instance, who was playing a xylophone, interpreted the poem as follows:

Waves lap gently on the seashore	Slow upward glides over six or seven notes.
Fishes dart	Fast upward glides over ten or eleven notes. Gaps between glides.
Black clouds bring a raging storm	Loud rapid succession of single notes using hands alternately.
Out peeps the sun and shines upon a rainbow	Gentle, slow succession of upward and downward glides, interspersed with isolated notes.
Waves lap gently on the seashore	As before, with a few downward glides.

But the combined effect of 27 pupils performing as individuals was that each line sounded much the same as the rest. As the pupils were concentrating on what they were doing, and apparently unaware of the overall effect, the teacher played them a recording of their performance, and invited comments. Stuart described it as 'rubbish'. Gradually, the pupils started to analyse the problems with the recorded piece: 'It sounds all the same'; 'It is too crowded'. In John Cage's terms, quoted at the start of this chapter, they had failed to integrate silence with sound. Silence seemed not to have been considered at all. John Cage's advice to a young composer of a 'busy' over-written score that 'there is not enough of nothing in it' would again have been appropriate. The class had concentrated on sound, and neglected silence. Suggestions about how the piece could be improved were made. Some pupils thought that there should be fewer performers. Others thought that some instruments were unsuited to particular lines, or that individuals were playing them in an inappropriate manner. The class rehearsed each of the lines again with pupils only joining in when they thought their instruments suitable. The pupils thought that this was an improvement, but had many ideas for further development. The sea music developed into a project to which the pupils returned at intervals over the next six weeks. By the end of this time, pupils were divided into four groups, one for each of the four different lines. Each group had developed their piece over several weeks, refined their choice of instruments, and, finally, notated the music so as to show its organization. Fig. 3 is a copy of the graphic score drawn by the *Fishes dart* group.

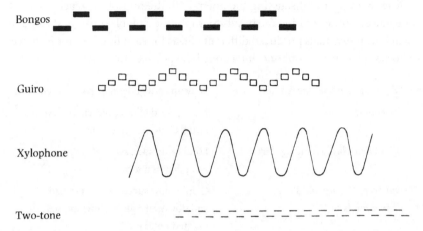

Bongos

Guiro

Xylophone

Two-tone

Fig. 3 *Fishes dart*. Each instrument has its own line, and a symbol which reflects the performer's perception of the shape of the single sound chosen. The four parts are staggered to show a progressive start and finish. The horizontal scale is not literal; there were many more sounds than are shown.

Stimulus 2: a published story

A term later, the same class had been listening to extracts from the *Narnia Chronicles* by C. S. Lewis. They decided to compose a piece entitled *The Creation of Narnia*. Initially, groups of pupils worked on segments of the story, and drew graphic scores which they stuck together in sequence. In other words, they started by organizing their composition like the finished version of the sea music. This time they were not satisfied; they wanted a continuous piece, not a series of chunks. At the pupils' request, and with their guidance, the teacher copied the individual scores onto a long sheet of paper, linking each group's work through the modification of beginnings and endings of sections. The class then determined the interpretation of the new score, drawing on the experience of the individual groups. The teacher coordinated the performance by moving a ruler along the score, which was more than 15 metres long (see extract, Fig. 4). At the start of the project, the pupils used classroom percussion instruments. Later they found it easier to achieve some of the effects they wanted with their voices. The final piece was almost entirely vocal.

Stimulus 3: a collection of instruments chosen by a teacher

At the end of the school year, the same class devised some 'machine music' to be included in a performance of John Paynter's *Space Dragon of Galatar*

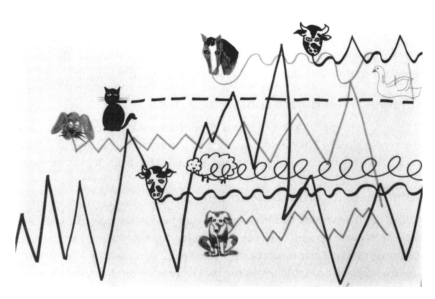

Fig. 4 An extract from *The Creation of Narnia*.

(Paynter 1972). The teacher offered a stimulus of three machines—an old 'banda'[5] machine, a photocopier, and a vacuum cleaner. The class listened to these, and then collected more machine music using improvised instruments such as rulers, abacuses, and rough paper which could be scrumpled and torn into shreds. Next the pupils discussed how to organize their piece so that even the quietest sounds could be heard. Eventually, the sounds were arranged according to their loudness, and introduced progressively with the quietest sound first. The piece ended when the teacher gave a signal for all the instruments to gradually run down.

Stimulus 4: a pupil's painting

Paul, aged 6, had painted a picture of himself standing outside his house. The sun was shining and the sky was blue. His teacher asked how he was feeling in the picture, and Paul said he was very happy. Would he like to make some 'happy' music to go with the picture? Paul chose a xylophone. He focused on

---

5 Prior to wide introduction of photocopying in schools, duplication of teaching materials was generally carried out using Banda machines. A single original could be used to make hundreds of copies, using a fluid that was based on alcohol. The copies were generated by rotating a drum using a handle that made a characteristic sound—hence its use in this composition. (For further information about Banda machines, see Wikipedia, http://en.widipedia.org/ wiki/Spirit_duplicator.)

five adjacent notes, choosing a dance-like rhythm. He finished with a glide along the whole length of the xylophone, moving from the bottom to the top. His teacher said that she had enjoyed his 'happy' music. Would he like to play some 'sad' music now? No, he would not. He was feeling very happy.

Stimulus 5: an object chosen by a pupil

Jana, aged 7, brought a seashell into school. Her friends passed it round, and observed it closely. They described it as cold, smooth, and curly. They made some cold, smooth, and curly sounds and assembled them into a piece of music.

Stimulus 6: a verbal description

A class of 10-year-olds had been working on pets in several subjects. They decided to make up a piece about a particular dog who had visited the class the previous day. Their teacher collected a list of words which described the dog: four-legged, brown, hairy, warm, barking, and so on. Next, she asked for suggestions of sounds to represent the words. 'Four-legged' was easy enough. Yoko chose a drum and hit it four times. But what would the pupils make of 'brown'? Darren volunteered to find a 'brown' sound. He chose a xylophone and tentatively played a few high notes. 'That's not brown, it's green,' said Yoko. Yoko then played a few quiet, slow, low notes on the xylophone, and all the pupils, including Darren, agreed that it was a superior 'brown' sound. The class continued through the list. Eventually, they had twelve sounds. Pupils took turns to play them whilst another pupil constructed a piece about the dog by conducting them, as in the Conductor game described in Chapter 2.

Stimulus 7: a piece of music chosen by a pupil

Katy, aged 9, had worked out how to play *Twinkle, Twinkle, Little Star* on an electronic keyboard, starting on the note C. She had taught it to her friend Sarah, and they were playing it together with Sarah starting on the highest C available, and Katy two Cs lower down. Their teacher suggested that Katy should work out another part to play, whilst Sarah played the tune. Katy started by playing her first note—the low C—all the way through. Eventually, she produced a slow-moving part based round low C, but with occasional, careful, use of the adjacent B and D.

Stimulus 8: a piece of music chosen by a teacher

A class of Year 2 pupils were working within the topic of Colour. Their teacher played them an extract from each of the movements of Bliss's *Colour Symphony* (1922) naming them, as Bliss had done, 'Purple', 'Red', 'Blue', and 'Green', respectively. The class then devised some 'Black Music' which they contrasted with some 'White Music'.

Stimulus 9: a piece of music motivated by the arrival of a new piece of software

A new piece of composing software—a multi-track sequencer—had just been installed, and two pupils, not known for their computer skills, had taken a particular interest in it. While the rest of the class continued with group compositions based on jazz, the two pupils used headphones to work separately from their peers as they explored sound colours, and ways of combining sound colours. At the end of the lesson, the whole class listened to some of the work that had been carried out using the software, and the two 'expert' pupils played some motifs, or germs of musical ideas, that they thought could be used as the basis of a class composition in the next lesson. The teacher, and class, agreed that this was a good idea that would be pursued. The teacher thanked the pupils for their input, and spoke of how she would organize opportunities for other pupils to try the software too.

With the exceptions of *Twinkle, Twinkle,* and the final example, the composing activities described above all involve the transformation of experience in some medium other than sound into music. In some cases, for instance the machines and the storm, there has also been transformation of sound into music. It is not always easy to transform experience in sound into music. One can end up just copying the sounds closely to produce sound effects, not music. This can result in an exceedingly disjointed product, particularly when poems or stories are involved. For example,

'He ran down the corridor'
(*Sounds of someone running down a corridor*)
'He slammed the door'
(*Sound of door being slammed*), etc.

This sort of work can be a first stage of production of a composition, but it has not got there yet. Although the ability to copy sounds is useful, and shows fine listening and performing ability, it is not, on its own, composing. Composing is about transformation, not translation. A piece of music is not judged by the extent to which it is an accurate copy of something else, but as a piece of art in its own right. There is room in music for sound effects. But they need to be used as part of the music, not as a replacement for it. An example of this is found in *The Creation of Narnia* (see p. 40). The score for the section on the creation of animals (see p. 41) illustrates the use which the pupils made of impressions of animal sounds. But the jagged line running through this section represents a musical idea—a rising and falling melodic pattern sung to 'Ah'—which was present through most of the piece. The animal sounds were part of the development of this idea. In other words, they contributed to the musical development within the piece.

Some established composers have also used sound effects to enhance a musical idea. The cuckoo effect in Delius's *On Hearing the First Cuckoo in Spring* is one example. Here, the effect is realistic enough for us to recognize that it depicts a cuckoo song. But the context in which it is set is impressionistic. It is not intended as an accurate copy of the sound and silence which typically accompany cuckoo song. It is a different quality of experience.

Popular music, too, uses sound effects. One example which pupils may be able to locate in their grandparents' record collection—possibly next to Grandad's old flared jeans—is The Move's *Fire Brigade* (1968). Vocal impressions of a (now superseded) fire-engine siren in the chorus complement an introduction by an apparently genuine fire engine. But the whole effect is nothing like that of a real fire engine racing to deal with an emergency. There is none of the panic, or danger, or relief that it is not your house on fire. The whole piece is, I think, a well-organized, and skilfully timed, joke.

Much music is free of association with any named stimulus: a story, a poem, lyrics, or a visual image. Think, for instance, of all the untitled sonatas and symphonies. Pupils can compose without an external stimulus too. When pupils spontaneously make up pieces at the music table, this is often what they are doing. They are not always depicting Winter, or telling the story of 'Goldilocks and the Three Bears'; they are stringing sounds together for the joy of it, or rather the sound of it. Often, however, an adult asks the composer what the piece is about, and the pupil supplies a title to please the adult.

Stimuli are useful devices for facilitating composing. Established composers, as well as pupils, use them from time to time. But we need to avoid the idea that music can be composed only in response to a stimulus, that it has to be about something or other. If we are not careful about the ways in which we use stimuli, pupils can lose the ability to work with sound for sound's sake. They can come to regard composing as a sort of reversible system for transmitting secret messages. The composer takes the stimulus and disguises it as a piece of music. The audience takes the piece of music, and guesses what the stimulus is. Seems a bit pointless, doesn't it?

Choice of materials

Earlier in this chapter (p. 27 and 29), we considered some uses of a range of materials: classroom percussion instruments, orchestral instruments, ICT, body sounds, and improvised instruments, for instance. A teacher's choice of materials depends on a number of factors: availability, suitability to the composing task in hand, pupils' experience, and so on. Often there is no point in restricting the materials available. But there are occasions when a teacher has a particular reason for offering the pupils a selection. Perhaps the teacher feels that a class that has become preoccupied with rhythm at the expense of melody would benefit from a period of working only on tuned instruments.

Should a teacher restrict the sounds that a pupil makes with a given instrument? Again, not for the sake of it. We have already considered this issue with reference to instrument technique (see pp. 28–9). It arises also in the context of the selection of notes available to players of tuned instruments.

Pupils are sometimes introduced to composing by playing tuned instruments with some of the notes removed. In particular, one will see pupils restricted to the notes C D E G A, or even just a subset of these notes. This five-note (pentatonic[6]) scale occurs in many musical contexts such as Hungarian folk song, Scottish song, and other styles of folk music. It forms the basis of two classic approaches to music teaching: Carl Orff's *Schulwerk*, and Zoltan Kodály's *Choral Concept*, both of which draw on pentatonic folk song. Used in such an authentic, or at least integrated, context, or even to produce a special effect, pentatonic composition can be worth while. However, pupils are sometimes restricted to this pentatonic scale for another reason: no combination of notes drawn only from this scale sounds violently dissonant to western ears.[7] I find this an unfortunate approach. First, pupils do not need to listen to what they are doing: everything will sound all right. Second, pupils are unable to reproduce some music they know; they cannot, for instance, play the melody of *Twinkle, Twinkle, Little Star*, or many popular songs. Third, pupils do not get a chance to play with dissonance and make their own decisions about whether to include it in their compositions. Pupils can be given all the notes in the western (chromatic) scale—the black and white piano notes—for many composing activities. And when they are using instruments, such as string

---

6 Any five-note scale (e.g. C D E F G), is pentatonic. The pentatonic scale referred to here (C D E G A) can be transposed to start on any note to give, for instance, F G A C D or G A B D E, or all the piano black notes: F# G# A# C# D#.

7 The semitone (e.g. the interval B–C, or C–C#), is both the smallest, and most dissonant, interval in the western scale. The lack of dissonance of intervals drawn from the pentatonic scale C D E G A stems from the absence of single semitone intervals within the scale. The intervals C–D, D–E, and G–A consist of two semitones, that is, one tone, and the intervals E–G and A–C consist of three semitones. Most pentatonic scales found in European folk song do not include single semitone intervals.

instruments, which can produce other intervals as well, why not let them explore non-western scales and the notes between semitones as well?

Responding to composing

Your response helps pupils to evaluate their work, and learn from it. It also helps you to understand what the pupils have achieved and learnt, and to decide what activity might be appropriate next. It is rarely appropriate just to thank pupils for their piece and move on.

The accounts of composing activities described earlier in this chapter give some examples of response to composition. Response takes three main forms: questioning, suggesting, and encouraging.

Questioning helps you to find out more about the composing process than you observed whilst the pupils were working:

- Why did the pupils start the piece that way?
- Did they reject any ideas?
- If so, on what grounds?

Questioning also helps the pupils to evaluate their work:

- Are they pleased with it?
- Why?
- Are there any parts which they think could be even better?
- How might they improve them?
- Are there any differences of opinion within the group?

Teachers can be reluctant to make *suggestions* for two reasons. First, there is the view that as composing is a creative activity, all the ideas should come from the pupils. Of course we must value pupils' ideas. But this does not mean that we should never tell them some of our own. We are employed to teach, not to observe, and teaching includes helping pupils to benefit from some of our more relevant ideas. In any case, much questioning is actually suggestion in disguise. For instance, the question, 'Do you think your piece of music is too short?' is asked typically by teachers who think that the piece *is* too short, and have ideas about how they would lengthen it, given the chance. Suggestion has its place; we just need to recognize when we are making suggestions, and when pupils are working things out for themselves.

Second, teachers may be reluctant to make suggestions in response to composition through concern that what they say may not be sensible. This is a particular worry for teachers who feel they are not familiar with the vocabulary that accomplished musicians use when talking about music. A suggestion given in plain English is not necessarily any poorer; it may well be superior, and is certainly more likely to be understood by the pupils. When you hear a piece of pupils' composition, you will usually think spontaneously of suggestions you could make. It can be helpful to draw parallels with an art form about which you do feel more confident to make suggestions. My initial thoughts about compositions are often similar to those about stories. Have the pupils worked out how to start? Have they worked out how to stop? These questions are not as simplistic as they sound. Young pupils often begin playing when you ask them to, and carry on until you ask them to stop. Having thought about the beginning and the end, what about the bit that comes in between? Is it going somewhere, or are the ideas disjointed, and not developed? Are there too many, or too few, ideas? Is the end a logical conclusion, a well-organized surprise, or a disappointment, as in a story which suddenly ends with 'and then we woke up and realized it was a dream' or 'and then we went home for tea'?

Other pupils can be drawn into discussion of composition. They often have pertinent points to make, and helpful suggestions to offer. They learn as composers from constructive criticism of the work of others. The composers may have set a poem by using different music for each line, with the result that the piece is a series of disparate chunks. How can that be resolved? Ask the pupils (see p. 134). Open discussion means that pupils' compositions can be compared, and it helps with listening too: 'What pattern did you play, Marco?' 'Did anyone else have a pattern like that, alternating between two notes with the same letter name?' 'Let's listen to Marco's group again, and check that we can hear his pattern.'

The third aspect of response is that of encouraging. There are times when questioning and suggesting are inappropriate: the pupils are doing very well on their own, and you just wish to encourage them to carry on.

We respond to pupils' composing partly because of our wish to see their work as part of a progressive music education. When listening to their work, we are always alert to ways in which we could promote progression. But this progression will not necessarily be accomplished through further revision of the same piece. Mozart did not continually revise the symphony he wrote at the age of 8. He did the best he could with it at that particular time and moved on, showing his progress through the music he wrote later. Sometimes, the most appropriate teacher response to a composition is simply the suggestion that the piece is now complete, followed by the offer of another stimulus intended to help the pupils' progress.

Questioning and suggesting make more sense if pupils can remember their composition. It is useful to record compositions onto CD, or using other media, as a matter of course. Recordings need to be made quickly and efficiently. The better the equipment, the more useful the recording will be. But a functional recording can often be made with a suitably sited ghetto-blaster with a built-in microphone. As well as assisting with immediate response to composing, recordings can be used as a record of pupils' achievements in music, and are a valuable resource when a teacher, or pupils, wish to reflect on progress made in music.

One final point about response to music. Music has its own meaning, not all of which can be expressed in words. When we talk about music, we comment only on parts of it. The whole is more than the sum of the parts. Thus a verbal description of a piece is never more than a pale copy of the original. Talking about music is valuable because it enables us to communicate some of our ideas. But it is never a substitute for the experience of music itself.

Notation

Notation is simply a means of recording a composition. There are many composing activities in which notation is not necessary because the composition is recorded in another way, for example it is remembered or stored on a CD. The machine music described on p. 41 was such a case.

Where we do wish to use notation, it needs to be of an appropriate form. In my long/short lesson (see p. 34), I chose a form of notation that reinforced the concept we were exploring. Staff notation, for instance, would have been inappropriate because we were not playing rhythms which could be notated conveniently by symbols such as crotchets and quavers.

The links between music and visual symbol are interesting and ambiguous; notation, like words, can never account for more than some aspects of music. But the relationship between music and symbol, like that between music and talk, can be exploited in the development of composing. The use of sound pictures, such as those given in Fig. 5, can help with the establishment of this relationship.

Sound pictures can be used to structure experimentation. Adults would probably have little difficulty thinking of a way of representing the first picture (Fig. 5a) on a tuned percussion instrument. Most would use a single beater to glide from the bottom to the top of the instrument and back down again, three times. For the second picture (Fig. 5b), many would choose a single pitch and either just play it once (if it sustained well), or repeatedly (if it did not). They would see the third picture (Fig. 5c) as a combination of the first two, and deal with it accordingly. The fourth picture (Fig. 5d) might provoke them to think about, and revise, the speed of the glides they made for the first and

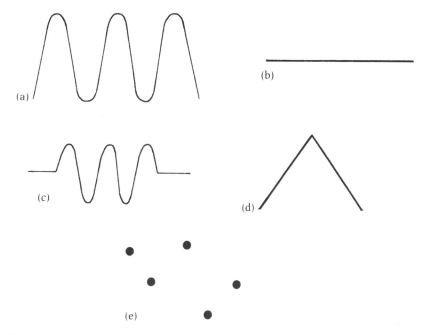

Fig. 5 Sound pictures.

third pictures. Replace the fourth picture with exactly the same shape drawn in red instead of black, and they would probably laugh politely. Colour is irrelevant, isn't it? They might not like the fifth picture (Fig. 5e) much at first sight, but, by using the system they have developed in which the picture is read from left to right as a graph of pitch against time, it can be interpreted as a single short highish note, followed by a lower one, a note higher than the first on, a very low one, and then a repetition of the second one to conclude.

Pupils, particularly young pupils who have not learnt to read music, often do not make these assumptions. They may choose to read from left to right, or from top to bottom, or may read the whole picture, or each shape, as a unit. They may vary loudness instead of pitch, or they may just draw the shape with their beater as they play up and down, seemingly at random. As in the piece about the dog (see p. 42) they may not have learnt that colour is irrelevant. (Is it?) Pupils' responses to the fifth picture are diverse.

We learn from this that there are many possible relationships between music and symbol. We may wish to make sure that pupils learn our adult relationship: this will eventually help them with staff notation which does read from left to right, and is, in a sense, a graph of pitch against time. But perhaps we can preserve the other relationships too. This is not because they are childish, but because the adult system is arbitrary. Other systems offer opportunities for different sorts of music. And as we observe the relationships that pupils establish between sound and symbol, there is much that we, as composers and teachers, can learn.

Facilities for music

As music consists of sound, it has particular requirements for facilities. Having several groups of composers within a classroom can create so much volume that it becomes difficult for pupils to hear the results of their own work. In fact, pupils seem much better able to cope with the competing noises than their teachers. This is probably because pupils are interested mainly in their own piece, whereas teachers have learnt to notice what is going on throughout the classroom.

Teachers can develop their tolerance. But alternative arrangements, also, can help. One solution is to use a larger room, such as the hall, if available. A second is to use more than one work area. For instance, you might arrange for a group to work in a cloakroom. Naturally, the feasibility of this suggestion depends on the arrangements for the supervision of pupils within your school. Third, you may prefer groups to compose in turn whilst the rest of the class are doing something else; perhaps art or mathematics. This arrangement can offer further advantages over the whole class composing at the same time. First, all groups have access to the entire pool of available instruments. Second, groups can work at their own pace; they do not all have to finish together. Third, compositions can be performed to the class individually. This can improve the quality of discussion considerably. With the best will in the world, it is very difficult for pupils to concentrate on a series of four or five performances, particularly if they are excited about their own.

Noise through the walls is another consideration. Some schools seem to have been designed without thought to the fact that music makes a noise, and yet requires quiet. In schools where music is valued, everyone accepts that they will overhear other classes making music from time to time. Naturally, there is give and take. Teachers need to know that there will be times of each day when they will not be disturbed by music. But this is not just a matter of music only taking place when neighbouring teachers have given their permission or are out. It really is give and take. A teacher at a primary school where music is thriving explained: 'Of course there are quiet times. But if a teacher in the classroom next door is doing a creative music lesson, you would not plan to do silent reading.'

In schools where music is not so well established, teachers may, initially, be less tolerant of the sounds of composing in the next room. One problem is that the combined sound of several groups composing can seem chaotic to a teacher on the other side of a wall. Indeed, it can sound as though the pupils are just messing around. Teachers convinced that pupils are working become more tolerant. Try inviting teachers into your room to *see* what is happening. Alternatively, take composing lessons in a room such as the hall which other teachers walk through. Include examples of pupils' composition at times of sharing, perhaps during assembly.

Early in my teaching career I took a composing lesson with a class of 11-year-olds. Each group was working purposefully and enthusiastically from a workcard, and I was really pleased with how things were going. Four groups were using classroom and orchestral percussion, and the fifth was using the inside and outside of the piano. In the next room was an experienced and very kind technology teacher mindful of the disruptive behaviour which probationary teachers can sometimes face. Clearly, he thought that I needed assistance, for he came into my teaching room with his cane. As he strode into the room, his face wore a firm, even fierce, expression. As he looked around him and saw the pupils sitting in their chairs, discussing their ideas, and trying them out on instruments, his expression changed to one of utter surprise. From his side of the wall, it had not occurred to him that the pupils were working. From my side, there was no doubt of it.

Chapter 4

Performing

. . . how can we expect to produce a vital performance if we don't re-create the work every time? Every year the leaves of the trees reappear with the spring, but they are different every time.

Pablo Casals in *Conversations with Casals* (Corredor 1956: 196)

The composers and performers of a piece of music are often the same people. They may have composed a piece with a view to performing it later. Or the composing and performing may take place at the same time, as in some types of jazz.

This chapter focuses, for simplicity, on activities in which pupils are interpreting music which is already composed. Thus we are at the second stage of the sequence

composing → performing → listening.

Teachers who are working with music in a relationship that looks more like

composing ⟶ performing ⟶ listening

music-making

will be able to work out, for themselves, how to apply this chapter to what they are doing.

Performing, like composing, is a creative process. The musician's frame of reference is different, for the composition is already there. But, to paraphrase Pablo Casals's statement, no two performances of the same piece are, or should be, identical.

Performers receive instructions from a composer, which they transform into music. But however these instructions are given—verbally, or through graphic or staff notation perhaps—they do not say all that there is to be said about the piece. An interpretation of a Chopin Prelude, for instance, in which the pianist just played the notes written and only got louder, softer,[1] faster, or slower in response to the composer's markings, would be dull, and not what Chopin wanted. In a sense, performers flesh out the bare bones of pieces devised by composers. Often, when performing, musicians focus on accurate interpretation of the composer's instructions. Accuracy is important. But it is not the be-all and end-all of performing. There is nothing slavish about performance. It can be every bit as exciting as composing.

In school, performing can take place on voices, instruments (including ICT resources), or a combination of these. I start with singing, and later add some instruments. I do not assume that teachers are able to accompany themselves on the piano, guitar, or any other instrument. Teachers who can do this will have no difficulty working out how to apply their skill in those songs and instrumental pieces which benefit from accompaniment.

Starting singing with children

While many songs can be learnt with the support of backing tracks, there are times when a teacher will wish to sing without using equipment, or where there are no backing tracks available.

Primary teachers vary in their confidence as singers. Some sing seemingly without a care in the world, regardless of the situation. But many are self-conscious about singing from time to time, or even all the time. There is nothing new about this. In 1597, Thomas Morley opened one of the earliest known music theory textbooks, *A Plaine and Easie Introduction to Practicalle Musicke*, with a self-styled non-singer's account of an embarrassing incident:

supper being ended, and Musicke books, according to the custome being brought to the table: the mistresse of the house presented me with a part, earnestly requesting me to sing. But when after manie excuses, I protested unfainedly that I could not: everie one began to wonder. Yea, some whispered to others, demanding how I was brought up. (Morley 1952: 9)

What did Philomathes, the speaker, do about this? Give up going out to supper? Claim to have perpetual laryngitis? No. The extract continues:

upon shame of mine ignorance, I go nowe to seeke out mine olde frinde, master Gnorimus, to make my selfe his scholler.

In other words, Philomathes determined to conquer what he perceived as a problem. Clearly, this fictional incident was set up by Morley. If Philomathes had not decided to take lessons, there would not have been much point in

---

[1] Some music educators prefer to speak of 'quiet', rather than 'soft', sounds. I prefer 'soft' because this is the term used generally when describing music outside school.

Morley writing his book. But there is a serious point to it. Singing can be developed. Many, possibly all, of those who claim to be unable to sing, or to sing with any confidence, can improve their ability. And although it is more straightforward to learn to sing as a child, it is possible at any age. There are plenty of examples of trainee teachers learning to sing confidently during teacher training, or teachers learning after several decades in the profession. One cannot learn to sing overnight, but, with sustained practice, it is possible.

Philomathes was not worried only about singing. The reference to the 'Musicke books' suggests that his concerns included singing unfamiliar melodies from staff notation: sight-singing as it is sometimes called. No one is born able to sight-sing. It is a skill which must be learnt, and is usually taught. Ideally, practice in sight-singing starts in youth, but there are plenty of adults who learn it. I doubt that sight-singing is beyond the reach of any teacher. However, a great deal of singing with pupils can take place without it. Sight-singers' only real advantage over everyone else is that they are able to learn new songs from books more quickly. There are plenty of other ways of learning new songs.

When planning singing with pupils, you can take your own initial confidence into account. You can organize singing so that you are faced only with challenges that you feel ready to meet. That way, your confidence will grow. And, as we shall see, there is no need for pupils to lose out when you organize their singing in such a way as to develop your own confidence.

Teachers often start singing with a new group of pupils by teaching them a song. Whilst this can work very well, it can be highly stressful for the teacher. It involves an element of leaping into the unknown. Will the pupils like the song I have chosen? Will they know it already? Will it be too difficult for them? Will I be able to teach it to them? We rarely operate like this in other areas of the curriculum. Usually, we find out what pupils are able to do, and plan accordingly. So consider starting singing with pupils by singing songs they already know. You will need to know them too. Ideally, learn them by sitting in when the pupils are singing with someone else. In any case, practise them before leading the pupils yourself.

If pupils are to make a confident start to a song, they need to know what note to start on, and when to begin singing. How will they get this information? A sung starting note is easier to copy than one played on an instrument, and is customarily given by the teacher. This can be the aspect of the singing lesson which is most intimidating to less confident singers. How will I know what note to sing? What if the note wobbles? In fact, you will probably find that if you know the song really well you will come out with a sensible note. Listen to the start of the song in your head before you sing it, and your starting note is more likely to be secure. But if you do not feel ready to sing a starting note alone yet, there are alternatives. Before the lesson, find a suitable starting note on an instrument such as a glockenspiel or keyboard. When the time comes to sing the song, play the starting note. If you feel up to singing it, do so. If you do not, ask the pupils to sing it, and join in, singing something like 'this is your starting note'. You will probably find that you only need to do this as a temporary measure, but even if you need to use a glockenspiel every time, the pupils will not suffer; they will be learning to take a note from an instrument.

There are many ways of actually starting the singing. Perhaps the easiest is to set the beat by clapping, and then, clearly, take a breath in time to start singing. If the pupils are watching you they will breathe with you and you will start together. Again, you will set an appropriate speed if you listen to part of the song in your head before you start. If all this sounds too much for you to begin with, just start singing, and the pupils will soon join in!

Singing with the pupils like this helps you to find out about the pupils' experience as singers, and means that your planning of future singing can be more effective. It helps you to become accustomed to singing *with* pupils before you need to sing *to* them. And it helps pupils to become accustomed to your voice. Pupils unused to singing with the 'changed voice' of a male teacher, for instance, will adapt much easier if they are singing a song they know.

One of the most important keys to successful singing with pupils is preparation. Nobody can successfully lead a song that they do not know properly, or they have not worked out how to start, or how to finish, or how to organize. Accomplished music teachers can seem to manage without preparation. In fact they are just displaying techniques which they have rehearsed to the point that they appear automatic.

Some accomplished music teachers may feel scandalized that I did not begin this section by teaching readers how to warm up their voices, and those of their pupils. I agree that it is very important to take care of our voices, for example by warming them up at the beginning of a session. However, requiring teachers to warm up their pupils' voices immediately before their first ever experience of leading a song can make this seem even more daunting. Warm-ups can be added as a teacher grows more confident. We cannot stop pupils singing at home without warming their voices, and a little more of that, at school, is unlikely to be harmful. Warm-ups can be sung badly, just as much as they can be sung well, and they can be as irrelevant to music-making as the worst chosen music games!

Choosing songs

How might we go about selecting songs for pupils? A song is a combination of lyrics and music. It can be helpful to start by considering these two dimensions separately.

When choosing a poem or story to read to pupils, thought about language level is second nature. If we want pupils to notice the words of songs, and to develop their language through singing, we need to be just as selective about lyrics. It is common, however, to find complex language in the songs that pupils sing. *The Miller of Dee*, a song included in radio broadcasts for schools on several occasions up to at least the mid-1980s, provided an example. It was a setting of Isaac Bickerstaffe's poem 'There Was A Jolly Miller'.[2] The first verse is as follows:

> There was a jolly miller once lived on the river Dee,
> He danced and sung from morn to night, no lark so blithe as he;
> And this the burden of his song forever used to be:
> 'I care for nobody, no, not I, if nobody cares for me.'

Were we to read this poem to pupils, we would, at least, talk through the meaning of some of this language. 'No lark so blithe as he' is not trivial. 'The burden of his song' has provoked some articulate adults to consult their dictionaries. In singing this song with pupils, we would, also, need to explain the meaning of these expressions. If this does not seem worth it, then it might be best to choose another song. The only nonsense songs pupils sing should be those written as such. Otherwise, there is a danger that pupils will switch off from the words altogether, and so miss out on an important dimension of the song.

Next, I turn to the music of songs. Pupils develop their singing through being challenged, but they need to be presented with material that is largely within their capabilities if they are to make any progress. This is just a special case of the general principle of matching the task to the child. The complexity of describing the melodic difficulty of songs is illustrated in the work of two Argentinian researchers, Silvia Malbran and Silvia Furno (Malbran and Furno 1987), who used 18 variables of pitch, rhythm, structure, and expression to draw up profiles of some 400 songs. We shall briefly consider just two musical aspects of songs: their melodic range, and their melodic shape, or contour.

Pupils have a small vocal range which is, generally, relatively low. Graham Welch (Welch 1979: 25) reports reference to this in a *Musical Times* article of 1890, but adds: 'the practice of fitting pupils' voices to the published repertoire, rather than the other way round, is still prevalent'. Images of choristers singing high melodies with enormous range seem to have masked the fact that pupils, left to their own devices, sing lower. This is illustrated by a comment of Iona and Peter Opie (Opie and Opie 1985: p. vi), the singing-game collectors referred to in Chapter 2, that 'children seem inclined to choose a rather lower pitch than might be expected—sometimes a little too low for comfort'. Even those experienced observers of pupils' song seemed to view

---

[2] This poem can be found, for example, in Untermeyer 1961.

pupils' choice of low pitch as deviance which needed to be justified, rather than evidence of a preferred low range. Pupils learn to sing in tune by singing in their comfortable range, and develop a wider vocal range by gradually extending it. So it is important that much singing takes place in this range. Vocal range is an important issue when we come to consider the development of pupils' singing. I raise it at this stage as reassurance to the considerable number of women teachers concerned that their singing voice is lower than the pupils'. Women teachers who think they have low singing voices usually find that their comfortable range is similar to that of pupils. Men teachers usually find that pupils are comfortable singing in a range an octave above them.[3] Sing songs at a pitch you find comfortable, and the pupils will probably be delighted.

Some melodies are much more awkward to sing than others. In general, melodies that leap around are harder than those that consist mainly of stepwise motion. This is partly because large leaps tend to take the melody out of the comfortable range, but also because they require considerable vocal control. The easiest way of assessing the difficulty of a particular melodic contour is to sing it yourself. And if you choose songs that you find straightforward, pupils will find it easy to follow you.

Another consideration when choosing songs is that of variety of content, musical form, and musical style. There are times—such as religious festivals or during work on particular topics—when it can be appropriate to sing a series of similar songs. And a teacher's repertoire of songs is likely to be stronger in some areas than others. But in the long term, variety in song is as beneficial as variety in reading matter and so forth.

In *Music from 5 to 16*[4] (DES 1985: 3), HMI suggested that the curriculum for those aged 5–7 should include opportunities to sing songs in the following categories:

- alphabetical, counting, sorting, cumulative songs
- nursery and folk songs

---

[3] An octave is the closest interval between two notes with the same letter name, for example, C. See also Chapter 7, n. 2 (p. 120).

[4] This chapter, in particular, refers on several occasions to this book, when considering government advice or expectations of music in schools. It was published before the National Curriculum for England, and takes a view of music education that is, in my opinion, timeless, visionary, and thoroughly musical. While several versions of the National Curriculum in England have come and gone, *Music from 5 to 16* (lightly updated in one's mind) has continued to provide a point of reference for many music educators. I refer to this book not because I have failed to read anything since 1985, which is emphatically not the case, but because I still admire its quality.

- singing games
- religious songs, some of which can be used in school assemblies
- modern, 'pop', and 'fun' songs.

Although it was published more than twenty years ago, this list remains relevant. The actual songs that teachers choose under these headings may have changed. But this list implies variety in form, content, and style. As younger pupils will often rely on their memories for recall, many suitable songs are very short. Nevertheless, the forms suggested are not confined to single short verses; repetition is used to generate songs with choruses, and songs which grow each verse (cumulative songs). Pupils who sing songs from all these categories will be singing for a variety of purposes: to reinforce language and mathematical concepts; during play and assembly; and as part of an explicitly musical experience. They will be learning traditional songs and adult songs, as well as those specially composed for schoolchildren. They will be learning songs that reflect the cultural range of pupils throughout the UK, and not only the cultural range of the pupils in their class.

This aspect of the curriculum strengthens in the list that HMI provided for older primary pupils. This is as follows:

- traditional folk songs and ballads
- songs from other lands and other cultures
- songs from former times
- modern songs including some 'pop'
- songs for all seasons
- songs for assembly
- simple descants, ostinati, and second parts in conjunction with the above
- rounds and canons
- music in and for drama.

(DES 1985: 6)

Teaching songs

There are many musical and efficient ways of teaching any song. When deciding how you will teach a song you have chosen, you will have in mind your knowledge of the pupils: their enjoyment of singing, likely concentration, and so on. There are two other factors to be considered:

- the structure of the song
- your previous experience.

Two aspects of the structure of the song may influence your choice of teaching method: its length, and the use of repetition. Long songs need to be subdivided in some way, or the pupils will be unable to remember them. Repetition within songs—for example a chorus—can be exploited to make learning more musical and efficient. If the pupils learn the repeating elements first, they become aware of the pattern within the song, and are able to sing substantial parts of it early in the learning process. Taking length and repetition into account, there are three main ways of organizing the learning of a song:

1. **Absorption**

   The song is repeated until the pupils know it. This can be an effective way of teaching very short songs.

2. **Segmentation**

   The song is divided into sections, for example lines, which are taught one at a time, usually in the order in which they appear in the song. The first verse of a song might be taught in this way.

3. **Segmentation + absorption**

   This is a combination of the two processes. Part of the song is taught through segmentation, and then the remainder is absorbed. With a song of several verses and a chorus, the chorus might be taught first, line by line. Then the teacher might sing the whole song, inviting the pupils to join in with the chorus. By the time that the end of the song is reached, the pupils may know the melody of the verse too. Teaching the pupils the words to some of the verses might be left to a later occasion; it is far better for pupils to know only one verse and be eager to sing all of them, than to know all of them and never want to hear the song again.

Ideally, lyrics are memorized during the learning process. Once pupils know them, they can concentrate on singing unhampered by reading. But this is not always feasible with long songs. A single large word sheet, or perhaps an overhead projection, is often preferable to many individual copies. Having the pupils look upwards, and in the same direction, can lead to better singing posture, and a greater sense of ensemble. For many songs, it is not necessary to write out all the words. A few key phrases or pictures can be enough to jog pupils' memory. Actions can also help with recall of words.

How might your previous experience affect how you teach a song? You will want to choose a procedure with which you feel you can cope. Below, I suggest a general procedure for teaching songs. At each of the three stages, I suggest options for those who do not feel confident to tackle the approach suggested. Implementing these options does not necessarily decrease the musical experience of the pupils. Their most significant disadvantage is that they require greater preparation, and so make less efficient use of teacher time. So there is something to be said for gradually learning to operate without some of the options, at least for some songs.

Stage 1 The teacher sings the songs to the children

This is so that the pupils know what they will be learning. Particularly when the song is to be taught through segmentation, this can increase motivation. It can be difficult for the teacher to appreciate the need for preliminary performance because he or she already knows the song.

OPTIONS

- Teach the song to a small group of confident singers in advance. Use them to support your singing.
- Arrange for another teacher, or a child, to provide a supportive accompaniment to your singing.
- Use an accompaniment that was recorded earlier.
- Sing along with a recording that includes the song as well as the accompaniment.

Stage 2 The teacher teaches the song to the children

Organize this through absorption, segmentation, or a combination of the two, according to the structure of the song.

OPTIONS

- As for any of the Stage 1 options.
- Use a recording that systematically teaches the song.

Stage 3 Everyone performs the song

This gives the pupils a sense that they have achieved something. With a long song, performances will be necessary at several points during the learning process.

OPTIONS

- Use the support of a supplementary accompaniment, as suggested for Stages 1 and 2.

Try to teach songs as a continuous piece of music, not as a series of disjointed phrases. This is particularly important if you decide to teach a song line by line. If you give clear instructions in advance, it is possible to go through a whole verse without stopping, or even interrupting the beat, as follows:

You sing line 1. Without a break, the pupils echo it.
Without a break, you sing line 2, and the pupils echo it.
And so on.

Consider the following alternative method of organizing line-by-line learning:

You tell the pupils that you are going to sing line 1.
You sing line 1.
You ask the pupils to echo line 1 after you have given a signal.
You give the signal, and the pupils echo line 1.
You tell the pupils that you are going to sing line 2.
You sing line 2.
And so on.

The only advantage of the second method is that it requires less initial organization by the teacher. On the other hand, it has the following disadvantages:

- It takes longer, and so is potentially more boring.
- The pupils do not find out how the lines fit together.
- The pupils have a greater opportunity to forget each line before echoing it.
- The beat is disrupted, with the effect that the feeling of participating in a continuous piece of music is lost.
- More complex signals are needed. In the first method, you can just point to yourself, or the pupils, when necessary and supply eye contact as appropriate. In the second method, you will need to provide a rhythmic signal, and also to sing starting notes for individual lines.

Teach words and notes together when you can. After all, you know both the words and the notes, and if you sing a verse to *lah*, or whatever, you probably still have the words going through your mind to help you. Eventually, you may find that some sequences of words or notes are so difficult that they need to be practised on their own. But by this stage, the pupils also will know how the words and notes fit together.

As soon as you think the pupils will be capable of getting through the song, or its first verse, let them have a go at it. Some problems may iron themselves out when you put the lines together, and segmented teaching mangles language in a manner that is best sustained for as short a time as possible. Whatever mistakes arise during the run-through, try to let the pupils continue for at least a few lines. Unnecessary stopping and starting disjoints the music, and some mistakes will correct themselves without the need for verbal instructions from you. Here, male teachers are at an advantage. As they sing an octave lower than the pupils, the correct model is always audible, even when some pupils are in error. Women's voices tend to get mixed up with the pupils'.

Above all, singing should be fun. Do not feel that you have to carry on singing a song until everyone is singing it perfectly. That time may never come. You can always try to smooth out some rough corners or teach another verse on another occasion. It is far better to have the pupils wanting to sing for longer, and eager to sing in the future, than to have them bored.

Developing singing

Singing must be enjoyable. If it is not purposeful, it soon becomes tedious. There are many respects in which pupils' singing can be developed: tone, control, vocal range, volume, expressive quality, and so on. Here we focus on developing one aspect of pupils' singing that has implications for all the others: the ability to sing in tune.

Many pupils have difficulty singing in tune. Quite how many depends, of course, on how you measure this. But Arnold Bentley (Bentley 1968), in a substantial questionnaire survey of British schools, found that roughly 25 per cent of 7-year-old boys and 11 per cent of 7-year-old girls were reported by their teachers to lack 'co-incidence at the unison'. By the age of 12, the figures for boys and girls had reduced to about 7 per cent and 1 per cent respectively. Bentley's investigation illustrates two patterns which have emerged in a range of studies. First, at any age, more boys than girls have difficulty pitching their voices. Quite why this is the case is not known. The difference in figures is too great to be accounted for solely by boys' so-called 'developmental lag': gender stereotyping is probably a contributory factor. Second, as pupils get older many learn to sing in tune. In other words, there are many schoolchildren for whom the problem seems to resolve itself. But can we help pupils to develop accurate pitching earlier? And can we do anything to help the substantial minority of pupils, particularly boys, who remain unable to sing in tune?

Pupils' ability to sing in tune often depends on what they are singing. In particular, much depends on whether the song lies within their comfortable vocal range. Try singing a song which is too high or too low for you. What happens to your tuning? As stated earlier, most pupils have a vocal range that is small and low. With practice, this range can gradually be extended. But whilst we are teaching pupils to sing in tune, it makes sense to choose songs that lie within their range. What might this range be? This is likely to depend on the previous experience of the pupils. Listen to pupils singing in the playground and notice the range they use. Cleall (1970) found that infant boys were most comfortable in an octave range of G to G across middle C. Young girls preferred a slightly higher and wider range: just over an octave from A to B. Many modern pupils' songbooks include songs in a suitable narrow, low, range.

How can you organize singing so that good pitch singing is developed? Clearly, it is not possible to devise a recipe that will work in all situations. But the following three principles may be helpful. First, pupils need frequent opportunities to sing. Singing need not be confined to singing lessons or even to songs: try singing the register, for instance. Second, singing needs to be organized as an activity which everyone participates in without a sense of embarrassment: each individual contribution, no matter how out of tune, is valued. Finally, pupils' individual progress in singing must be monitored. This is impossible if singing is organized only as an activity for large groups, for example two or more classes. Massed singing from time to time can be a marvellous social and musical experience. But, on its own, it is unlikely to do much to develop the vocal accuracy of those pupils who need special help. There is just no time to identify individual need, let alone respond to it.

How can we help pupils who still do not learn to sing in tune? There are three straightforward things we can do. First, we can check that the low range in which we are singing is comfortable for these pupils. Ask a child to sing a note of her or his choice, and see if it falls within the range. If it does not—and it is more likely to be below the range you are using—sing in this child's range some of the time. Second, we can ensure that the poor pitch singers are not all bunched together, unable to hear anyone who is in tune. This is not just a bit of social engineering, but a way of helping them with their singing. You may have had the experience of finding your singing becoming more relaxed and more accurate when you are next to a good singer, partly through resonance. Third, if pupils are aware of their difficulty, we can encourage them to think about it with optimism. Rather than saying something like 'Never mind, we can't all be good at everything, and you are good at running', we can point out that pupils develop at different rates in all sorts of ways—for instance some are taller than others—and that their singing will develop as they get older. In the meantime, they need to be given many opportunities to sing. Nobody ever learnt to sing in tune by not singing at all.

Vocal accuracy, though important, is only one aspect of singing. Nobody—teacher, parent, or child—should become obsessed with it. It is untrue that anyone who cannot sing in tune is necessarily 'unmusical'—whatever that means. An accurate singer demonstrates fine pitch hearing; an inaccurate singer may have just as fine hearing, but have poor control of the vocal mechanism. So the use of the term 'tone deaf' to describe someone who sings out of tune is inaccurate. Some years ago, I met Andrew, a 6-year-old who had been rejected from a neighbourhood choir because of his poor pitching. According to his score on my Pitch Test (Mills, 1988a), his ability to observe the difference between pairs of notes which were very close in pitch was unusually high. Indeed, it exceeded that of all the 250 other 6- to 8-year-olds whom I tested. Clearly, Andrew was not tone deaf. In fact he was an unusually determined little boy. He wanted to get into that choir, and his parents had overheard him trying to teach himself to sing in tune by matching his voice with piano notes. By the time he was 9, he was reported to be singing in tune, and to be a promising trumpeter. But not all pupils have Andrew's persistence or opportunity. It is important that we do not write off developing singers as unmusical.

Last, a brief word about the development of two other related aspects of singing: breathing and volume. Pupils' breathing during singing can be guided from the earliest stages of development. Breathing at the ends of phrases produces a melodic flow which makes pitching easier, and, of course, preserves the meaning of the lyrics. As pupils learn to control their breathing, they become more able to sing long phrases without a break. But it is possible to place so much emphasis on the technicalities of breathing that singing becomes more aligned with PE than music. In the earliest stages of singing, it can be sufficient for the teacher to set a model of breathing at sensible points, and to draw the pupils' attention to this.

Concerning volume, it is not uncommon to overhear pupils being harangued for not singing loudly enough. Yet when they try to sing louder, they end up just shouting. Young pupils' voices are, by nature, quiet. Apparent volume can be increased by encouraging pupils to look up. Actual volume develops with age, but can be accelerated by good posture—an upright seated or standing position—and attention to breathing.

Writing songs for children

The Runaway Seed

The runaway seed fell into the ground and it grew, it grew.
The runaway seed fell into the ground and it grew, it grew.
The runaway seed fell into the ground
Off the tree with a leap and a bound
And it grew, grew, grew, grew, grew.

A little white shoot looked up at the sun and it grew, it grew.
A little white shoot looked up at the sun and it grew, it grew.
A little white shoot looked up at the sun
So now the tree had really begun
And it grew, grew, grew, grew, grew.

The rain came down and watered the tree and it grew, it grew.
The rain came down and watered the tree and it grew, it grew.

The rain came down and watered the tree
Then it was bigger than you and me
And it grew, grew, grew, grew, grew.

The ginormous tree reached up to the sky and it grew, it grew.
The ginormous tree reached up to the sky and it grew, it grew.
The ginormous tree reached up to the sky
Its branches stretched from side to side
And it grew, grew, grew, grew, *GREW*.

Sally Crane

The Runaway Seed, as you probably became aware as you read it through, is an alternative set of lyrics for the song *The Runaway Train*.[5] Sally Crane wrote these words following a fruitless search through songbooks for a song which tied in with some work on seed growth which she was leading with 7–8-year-olds.

There are many situations in which there is no song to fit our purpose. We can spend ages hunting through the indexes of songbooks to no avail. All the songs on our subject are slightly off the point, or the range is enormous, or the language is archaic. Writing our own song is a real alternative. And, of course, songwriting does not need to be left to those occasions when no suitable song is available.

As we have seen, songwriting need not start from scratch. You can write lyrics to fit a melody you know, or a melody to fit a suitable poem. Pupils can be involved, or even do all the songwriting. They often make up their own words to songs, so why not make the most of their enthusiasm? There are many feasible approaches. Sally Crane started by singing through *The Runaway Train* and letting the words take shape. This meant that the words developed in a pattern which suited the melody. *The Runaway Seed* is not the greatest poem since Wordsworth, but the fit of the words and music is excellent, and the pupils were thrilled that it had been written especially for them.

When making up a song, just let your ear be your guide. If you like the melody and it is easy to sing, and the words seem to fit well, it is likely to be successful.

Voices and instruments

Many songs are effective on their own; others sound more complete with the addition of some form of instrumental accompaniment. This can take many forms according to the nature of the song, the musical expertise of the teacher and pupils, and the availability of instruments. Often, the most effective accompaniments are very simple: complicated ones quickly swamp the song. Judge by ear whether or not an accompaniment is suitable.

---

5 *The Runaway Train* by Carson Robison and Robert E. Massey is in Carson Turner 1988.

Music from 5 to 16 (DES 1985: 6) includes this objective for 11-year-olds: 'Accompany singing on tuned or untuned instruments by playing remembered rhythms, melodic phrases, drones, repeated chord sequences and added parts.'

How might we add these types of accompaniment to a song? It is unlikely that you would wish to include all these devices simultaneously in a song, as this would probably make it very cluttered. But you might wish to experiment with a few, or possibly include different combinations in different verses. You will have your own ideas, and so will the pupils, but here are a few of mine. I take *Three Blind Mice* as my example simply because it is a song that all readers are likely to know. My full arrangement of the song is shown as Fig. 6. Below, I describe the types of accompaniments I have added to the melody.

Remembered rhythms

Rhythms derived from that of the song itself help to ensure that the accompaniment sounds part of the song. Repetition of the rhythm of the words 'three blind mice' (tbm) on a woodblock throughout the song can sound effective and also have a stabilizing effect. The same is true of 'see how they run' (shtr), which might be played on a drum. Consequently, I have combined these rhythms as an introduction to the song. After three 'three blind mice', 'see how they run' enters. And after two 'see how they run(s)', everyone starts singing. At the end of the song, the instruments continue for a little while. 'All ran after the farmer's wife' is a harder rhythm, which I have chosen to leave out for the present. I might add it when the pupils have mastered their parts as shown.

Drone[6]

Let us assume that we are starting the song on the note E. This means that we are in the key of C.[7] So the note C can be used as a drone, or the chord of C can be used as a drone chord (see Chapter 7, pp. 120–1 for an explanation of

---

[6] A drone accompaniment consists of a single low note (or possibly a single low chord) which is sustained throughout the melody.

[7] How can you work this out? Melodies nearly always end with their key note, so sing the song through, starting on an E, and check that it finishes on a C. It is safer still to take the key from the chord you would use to accompany the final note. Check that the chord of C makes sense with the final note of this song by playing it on an instrument such as an electronic keyboard. Published songs often have chord symbols written above the music; try taking the final chord as your key chord. Just occasionally, for instance when a song moves through several keys, this system breaks down. This is rare amongst songs in children's songbooks.

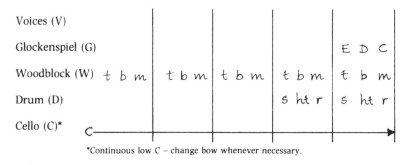

*Continuous low C – change bow whenever necessary.

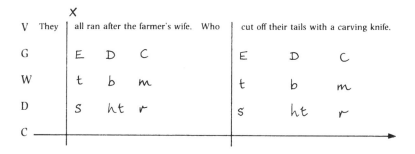

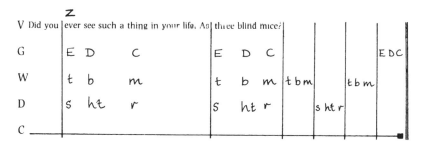

Fig. 6 Arrangement of *Three Blind Mice*.

chords). Drones can be played on any low instrument, such as a bass xylo-phone, but are particularly effective when played on an instrument that sustains well, such as a cello. C is one of the notes of the open strings on the cello, so this drone could be played by a cellist in the earliest stages of tuition. But the cello does need to be in tune if it is to be played with another instrument, such as a keyboard!

Melodic phrases

As the pupils are to remember their parts, I want to keep them simple. Like rhythm, melodic phrases can often be derived from the melody. The phrase 'three blind mice' (notes E D C) can be repeated throughout the song. The same is true of 'see how they run' and 'all ran after the farmer's wife' but I have chosen to include just 'three blind mice', on a glockenspiel, in my arrangement.[8] I have introduced it before we start singing so that we will be able to take our note from it.

The arrangement given in Fig. 6 is just one, simple, way of performing *Three Blind Mice*. I have resisted the temptation to include absolutely everything I could think of. The repeated chord sequence C G C to the rhythm of the words 'three blind mice' would, I thought, make the arrangement sound cluttered. Other parts, suggested by pupils or teachers, could be added, and some of mine left out. The song can be sung as a two-part or four-part round if subsequent parts start at the points marked X, Y, and Z. And if you wish to go further still, note that *Frère Jacques*, starting on C, can be sung simultaneously with *Three Blind Mice*.[9] Songs that fit together like this are sometimes known as *partner songs*. As these two partner songs are both four-part rounds, the possibilities for variety are enormous. You could use word rhythms or melodic patterns from either song in your accompaniment, sing the two songs simultaneously as rounds, or make up added parts which draw on both songs.[10]

Structures such as we have considered for arranging songs can, of course, also be used to arrange pieces for instruments alone.

---

[8] Each line of *Three Blind Mice* can be repeated to form a melodic accompaniment because the song is a round. With other songs, judge by ear whether or not this approach is successful.

[9] To establish the pace at which you should sing *Frère Jacques* to fit with *Three Blind Mice*, note that the rhythm of 'dormez-vous?' is the same as that of 'three blind mice'.

[10] Try, for instance, repeating the melodic phrase 'Frère Jacques, three blind mice' (C D E C, E D C).

What about staff notation?

Staff notation is simply a means of recording some types of western music. It is not a code that must be understood before any purposeful musical activity can take place. Some jazz musicians, and pupils learning the violin according to the Suzuki method, for instance, cannot read music. Some twentieth-century composers, including Luciano Berio, have occasionally found other forms of notation more appropriate to their purposes. And many musical traditions, such as many Indian traditions and much gamelan music, make little or no use of any written notation, let alone staff notation. Thus the study of written notation is not relevant to all forms of music-making, and much worthwhile musical activity in any musical tradition can take place without recourse to it. Some music is not staff-notatable; other music is not notated.

Consequently, pupils need not be taught to read music until they are ready to use it. And once they have learnt it, it need not become the only way of recording or accessing music. Pupils who have learnt to read music in conjunction with piano lessons, for instance, still benefit from opportunities to compose by ear at the piano, and on other instruments. There is a parallel here with written and spoken language. Pupils do not learn to read and write until they have been speaking for some time. And once they have learnt to read and write, they do not stop talking to each other.

When are pupils ready to learn to read music? This depends on the music curriculum in their school, their musical experience outside school, and their own pattern of musical development. In *Music from 5 to 16* (DES 1985: 3), HMI stated that 7-year-olds should have had:

musical experiences which should enable them, with varying degrees of skill and understanding, to . . . associate sounds with symbols; to show a readiness to see the relationship between performed music and various forms of notation (pictorial, graphic and conventional).

In the curriculum documents of some Local Authorities (LA), pupils are introduced to simple notation, including staff notation, by the time when they are about 8. But, in all cases:

♦ Music reading should be preceded by extensive experience of composing, performing, and listening without notation.

♦ Pupils should not be introduced to music reading before a musical need has arisen.

♦ Musical activity without notation should continue at all levels.

Teachers are not required by the National Curriculum to teach staff notation to primary pupils, but can of course teach it to pupils who are ready for it.

Saika and Shazia do not read music at all, but show awareness of a potential relationship between sound and symbol by referring to staff notation whilst they improvise on recorder and glockenspiel.

In *Music from 5 to 16*, the theme of *the sound before the symbol* is extended even to instrumental tuition, an area of school music in which notation has been introduced traditionally at an early stage:

Those who show the aptitude to learn recorders, violins and guitars may advantageously begin to play by ear and imitation; however, as and when there is a need for notation, it should be made available to them. (DES 1985: 5)

A consensus that many pupils are ready for the early stages of music reading after about two years of sustained classroom music seems to have emerged. This means that some 7-year-olds who have had systematic music education since their reception class may be reading music a little. But a teacher who takes over a class of 10-year-olds who have not had sustained musical experience is unlikely to find them ready to read music before they move into secondary school.

Because music reading is not introduced until pupils are ready, any class will include pupils at different stages of music reading. Those who do not yet read music benefit from having written music available, just as pupils who have not learnt to read the written word benefit from access to written language.

Even where pupils have learnt to read music, music reading forms only a small part of their classroom music. Amongst over a page of objectives for 11-year-olds in *Music from 5 to 16*, the only references to notation are contained within points about composing and performing:

In the school orchestra, the relationship between sound and staff notation has become explicit.

make a permanent record of such compositions by means of a tape recorder and/or the appropriate musical notation . . . play by ear and perform simple pieces (both notated and otherwise) individually and as a member of a group. (DES 1985: 6)

Pupils in the early twenty-first century may be able to use equipment more sophisticated than a tape recorder when they are making their recordings! But the point is that the use of notation follows from music-making, which continues without it at least some of the time. Thus the sound precedes the symbol.

Performing from staff notation is only one mode of performing: pupils who perform only from it are musically deprived. Teachers who do not read music can lead a valuable range of performing activities with pupils throughout the primary phase. That said, most teachers do not find music reading difficult, given sympathetic help. It can be worth getting to grips with it, if only to demystify the whole matter.

Responding to performing

In Chapter 3, I wrote of three modes of responding to composing: encouraging, suggesting, and questioning. The same modes of response apply also to performing. Encouraging needs no further comment. Traditionally, much response to performing—both outside and inside schools—has been suggesting, rather than questioning. A conductor of an orchestra or choir is likely to view the interpretation of a piece of music as his or her business, rather than that of the collective membership of the ensemble. Thus the conductor will tend to issue instructions about interpretation, rather than ask individuals for their opinions.

This autocratic role of the conductor is open to question. Hans Keller held the view that conductors are often dispensable. After all, much of the music they conduct was written for conductor-less ensembles:

The conductor's existence is, essentially, superfluous, and you have to attain a high degree of musical stupidity in order to find watching the beat, or the conductor's inane face for that matter, easier for the purpose of knowing when and how to play than simply listening to the music. But such established, collective stupidity is the conductor's very lifeblood, and it must be admitted that his attempts to maintain it at a steady level in order to justify his existence, his quick and skilful suppression of any sign of intelligence, let alone independent thought, have proved brilliantly successful . . . Under the influence of the conductor, orchestral playing has, in short, become an unmusical occupation. (Keller 1987: 23)

Hans Keller intended to be provocative. Yet he was making a serious point. Performers who are automatons are not musicians. Thus we need to encourage pupils to respond to their own performance:

— This is a happy song. Did it sound happy?
— Do you think an audience will be able to hear the words?
— Did it get fast enough?
— Did any of the instruments sound too loud?

It can be difficult to answer questions about the overall sound when you have been in the midst of the performance. Listening to recordings can help. Alternatively, pupils can be divided into two performing groups, and invited to respond to each other's performance.

That said, there is still a need for suggesting. It is right for a teacher to share her or his greater experience with pupils. Rehearsals in which everyone always had their say would be interminable. And when opinions are divided, someone has to decide how to move forward. My point is simply that pupils can be involved in the assessment of their own performing.

One area in which teacher-suggestion becomes very important is that of deciding when an item has been rehearsed sufficiently. The adage 'practice makes perfect' is not universally valid. A teacher is usually in the best position to anticipate when the point of over-rehearsal is about to be reached. Indeed, some performances are best viewed as one-off, and not rehearsed at all.

Performing for an audience

Up to now, we have thought about performing as an informal activity taking place within the classroom. But performing, traditionally, also forms a significant part of the public presentation of the school through concerts, entertainments, carol services, and so on.

Working towards public performances can be a worthwhile musical experience for pupils. It can develop social skills, and enjoyment in social activity. The achievement of high standards can lead to personal satisfaction. But working towards public performances can also be boring and irrelevant. Ordinary musical activity of composing, performing, and listening may be suspended whilst several weeks' work on some rather unattractive and perhaps very high songs takes place. The pupils may reach the best standard of which they are capable, given the material, days or weeks before the performance, and rehearsals may degenerate into a tirade about 'trying hard' and 'looking at me'. The value of pupils' individual contributions may be forgotten, and pupils with poor vocal accuracy may be asked to sing more quietly, stand behind a pillar, or play a drum instead.

The most useful public performances grow out of the music curriculum: they do not cut across it. They offer a public window into what would have been happening anyway, but provide pupils with an incentive to polish and focus their work. This is possible if the performance is conceived as an opportunity to show the public what pupils can do, rather than to use the pupils as a vehicle for public entertainment, and showing what teachers can do. Fortunately, child-centred performances often do entertain parents, and reflect well on teachers.

Attendance at child-centred performances can help to bring parents in touch with what their pupils are doing in music at school. Parents often had a rather uncreative music education themselves, and may, quite understandably, think that nothing has changed if end-of-term performances consist of performances of published pieces directed from the piano by a teacher. Inclusion of pupils' compositions, or items directed by pupils, can help parents understand the aims of the school music curriculum. Of course, some parents may experience a little initial resistance to change. The following passage is drawn from two letters which a teacher received after a secondary-school concert that included pupils' compositions as well as works by more established composers:

A veritable mish-mash of the sublime to the rediculous [*sic*] . . . A brief 'straw pole' [*sic*] amongst other parents following the concert indicated a general feeling of disappointment . . . I did appreciate the lovely plants as a backdrop but wondered what they thought of some of the music . . . This was *not music*, and it was a disgrace to have this offered to an intelligent well-intentioned audience, who come to be fed with *good* morsels . . . an excessive amount of experimental tinkling from the classroom groups, totally inappropriate fiddling with 'Japanese' electronic 'gadgets', and 'pop' drivel aimed at intellectual ankle level.

You can't win 'em all!

Chapter 5

Listening

Why is it difficult for so many people to listen? Why do they start talking when there is something to hear? Do they have their ears not on the sides of their heads but situated inside their mouths so that when they hear, something their first impulse is to start talking?

John Cage in *Silence* (Cage 1962: 48)

Now we move to the final stage of the sequence

composing → performing → listening

to consider activities which commence as listening. Listening is implicit in composing and performing. But our main concern here is listening to music that is already composed, and is performed by others. But before we can embark on this, we must clear up some difficulty which has arisen in the vocabulary used by some music educators.

Listening versus hearing

There is a sense in which listening and hearing are synonyms. 'Did you hear what I said?' can mean the same as 'Did you listen to what I said?' The questioner is not just attempting to establish whether a package of sound waves has been received; she or he wants to know whether its meaning, or significance, has been registered. But there is another sense in which the meanings of *listening* and *hearing* are less similar. Hearing can be a passive act of perception, a form of reception, whereas listening always involves concentration, focus, or activity on the part of the listener: 'Did you hear the birdsong?' 'Did you listen to the birdsong?' Because birdsong is something that we can either treat as background, or engage with, 'hear', in this context, could be taken to be synonymous with 'notice', not 'listen to'. The overlapping meaning of the words listening and hearing is a problem to music educators because they traditionally view the active sort of aural perception as their business, and the passive alternative as something that they wish, at least, to discourage. This verbal ambiguity has resulted in the introduction of some more obscure vocabulary to the music education literature. In *A Basis for Music Education* (1979), and also in later books, Keith Swanwick wrote of the musical processes of composition, performance, and audition. In the National Curriculum, there is reference to appraising (DfEE and QCA 1999a). Various writers have coined the verb 'to audience'. Others have referred to 'active listening'. I take the view that as all listening is active, there is no need for any prefix. I use the word 'listening' when I want to focus on active aural perception, and the words 'passive hearing' when referring specifically to the passive sort. Use of 'to hear' without qualification is in accordance with common English usage.

Music education is about active engagement with music; listening is part of music education. But what about passive hearing? It is not part of music education, but should it even be part of education? Should music be used as background in school at all? Background music is commonplace outside school. In the words of Terence Trent D'Arby: 'Music has become just another lifestyle accessory.' Roger Buckton (Buckton 1988: 62) describes it as 'wallpaper[ing] our acoustic environment'. Wallpaper is something that you cease to notice after a while unless, of course, you loathe it. If we accept the validity of Buckton's metaphor, then there are two reasons why background music is inappropriate to school. First, it irritates some people. Second, its presence reinforces the habit of not noticing sound, thus making the development of listening even more difficult. Children who cannot listen, cannot engage in music, and they miss out on many other learning opportunities too.

This means that music in school has to be something special, something we notice. Whenever music is played to us, we attend to it. Music in assembly should be something we listen to, not a background for notices, or walking in and out. Music in art should be there as a stimulus, not because the sound of silence is uncomfortable. And pupils should learn, at least some of the time, to give music their full attention. Listening need not always be accompanied by doing something else: dancing, drawing, or writing. Music is not just a stimulus for other activity; it is an aesthetic experience in its own right.

This means that music in school will be essentially different from many pupils' experience of music at home. This is not necessarily a bad thing. There are many ways in which we already make conscious decisions to make a school environment different from home. We do not, for instance, often decorate classrooms by wallpapering them; we change displays frequently so as to create a visual environment that is perpetually stimulating.

Listening across the curriculum

In the first edition of this book, I wrote of Fuwad, aged 8, who was spending his choosing time in the listening corner of his classroom. He had chosen a cassette of a story from a selection of recordings that included songs and other music. As he was listening through headphones, he did not distract others, and was not disturbed himself. Provision of a second headset meant that Fuwad could, if he wished, have a friend listening with him. He started and stopped the cassette, and controlled the volume, himself. Some weaving on display in the listening corner reflected the fact that the class were working within a topic of Fabrics. All around Fuwad, pupils were knitting, looking at fabric through a microscope, composing, writing, and doing mathematics. Some of the cassettes tied in with the topic; others did not. Later, Fuwad made a record of his listening on the class chart.

Fuwad's class teacher believed that the ability to listen was built up in all subject areas, not just music. Listening to stories, and other pupils speaking, for instance, could help to build up the concentration on sound that listening to music requires. Often, the pupils would listen to stories and music as a class. But independent listening was important too. The listening-corner environment was conducive to private, focused, listening. By checking the class chart, Fuwad's teacher learned which pupils were choosing to listen, and which needed some special encouragement.

Listening can take place at any time; it does not require special listening material. Ask a class to sit in what they think is silence for a minute or so, and then list the sounds they notice. They are likely to include many sounds that they would usually have ignored. Often pupils will notice these sounds again, even when you have not asked for silence. Listening material need not be either language or music. Try asking pupils to identify household or environmental sounds that you have recorded. Invite pupils to bring in recordings of sounds for others to identify, suggesting, perhaps, that a sign of success will be making a recording that others *can* identify.

A vocabulary for talking about music can be developed through listening to, and talking about, individual sounds and short sequences of sounds. Often, these sounds will be produced by the pupils themselves, perhaps when they are experimenting with instruments (see pp. 31–2). Once concepts such as pitch (high/low), dynamics (loud/soft), duration (long/short), and tempo (fast/slow), have been learnt in an unambiguous setting, they can be applied to substantial pieces of music. But talk about music need not be limited to these rather clinical terms. There is plenty of room for personal response to music; for words chosen by teachers and pupils, such as 'warm', 'bright', or 'scary'.

Listening to sound and language helps with listening to music, but is no substitute for it. Neither is it something that needs to be mastered before listening to music can commence. Pupils can listen to music from their first day in school. Listening to sound, music, and language are mutually enriching experiences.

The child as listener

What music is particularly suitable for pupils to listen to? When visiting primary schools, I often hear popular music or recorded extracts from well-known so-called classical orchestral works: Vivaldi's *The Four Seasons*, Saint-Saëns' *The Carnival of the Animals*, Holst's *The Planets*, Tchaikovsky's *The Nutcracker Suite*, for instance. Usually, pupils show evidence of enjoying this music. But there is a lot more music out there waiting to be enjoyed. We could play music from any period, from any culture, written for any combination of voices and instruments.

Why is it comparatively rare for pupils to be played the music of a non-western culture, or that of a living so-called serious western composer, for instance? Teachers often choose popular music, and the music of Mozart, Tchaikovsky, and so on, because they think that pupils will find it particularly easy to listen to. Why? Often, teachers are generalizing from their own adult experience. They find this music easy to listen to, and so they think that pupils will too. In fact, young children are more broad-minded listeners than we may imagine. Their taste for music is less predictable than we might suppose. We might think that pupils would prefer a movement of Mozart's *Eine Kleine Nachtmusik* to part of Stravinsky's *Rite of Spring*, or Acker Bilk's *Stranger on the Shore* to a number by some successor to the Modern Jazz Quartet, for instance. And we may be right. But we could, quite easily, be wrong.

When we say that we find some music easy to listen to, we are really saying that we know how to listen to it. We have learnt to listen to it, or music like it, over many years. We know what to expect. It is as though we have acquired spectacles through which the music we know is seen clearly. Young children have not had a chance to build up this same degree of experience yet; their response to music can surprise us. They can respond intuitively to any music.

By educating pupils in music, we help them to find structure and pattern in music, to hear what we hear. Provision of the closed sort of listening diet I have mentioned is well intentioned. Teachers want pupils to find and pursue individual tastes. How better to start than by offering pupils the music that teachers like? But pupils who also keep alive the ability to response intuitively to unfamiliar music remain unprejudiced listeners with greater capacity for future enjoyment of music. How can we preserve the intuitive response? Providing a wide range of listening material in school from an early age can help. Pupils who are aware of the diversity of music understand that the music they enjoy is just one part of a vast potential experience. They do not view the music they do not know, or do not care for, as *not-music*. They use spectacles, not blinkers.

Sam Taylor (1973) found that the music of a group of twentieth-century composers—Hindemith, Stravinsky, and Schoenberg—was more popular amongst 7-year-olds than 11-year-olds. Lizzie Lloyd (2007) has written of pupils' compositions based on music of Ligeti that grows from clusters of sounds.[1] Stravinsky's comment that his music 'is best understood by pupils and animals' is perhaps not as flippant as it sounds. Taylor found that adult tastes in music were well established by age 11. So if pupils are to remain broad-minded listeners, action in primary school is necessary. We need to provide a varied listening diet from pupils' earliest days in school. All music can be approached intuitively on its own terms. It does not have to be approached through an understanding of the music that went before.

We are not dealing with a new problem. Adults have often had difficulty in accepting contemporary or unfamiliar music. Plato wrote, in Book 4 of *The Republic*:

The introduction of novel fashions in music is a thing to beware of as endangering the whole fabric of society, whose most important conventions are unsettled by any revolution in that quarter. (Cornford 1969: 115)

Taylor reported only pupils' responses to so-called classical music. But I would guess that he would have observed a similar pattern if he had played examples of the music of non-western cultures to the predominantly white European pupils with whom he was working. There is a case for playing music that originated in non-western cultures in all primary schools. As well as offering pupils wider musical opportunities, this might help to erode the widely held adult view that there is something superior about western music, or the western musical scale. Arguments that this scale is determined by the laws of physics are bogus. Western use of this scale is largely accidental, and western preference for it is simply cultural.

Choosing music

There is no music which should not be played in primary school because it is too difficult. So how might we choose music for pupils?

---

[1] Lizzie Lloyd introduced pupils to the music of Ligeti by playing them a recording of his composition *Atmosphères*. A 'sound cluster' is exactly what it sounds to be. Put one of your hands down on a keyboard, with your fingers and thumb, and you have a sound cluster consisting of five notes. Move your hand up by a note, and you have another sound cluster. And so on. In a composition, the clusters may be close together, as in this example, or they may be more widely placed.

Some live music is chosen simply because it is available. Live performance is more exciting than recorded performance; it is often expedient to accept almost any that is offered. Secondary-school pupils and parents are often prepared to play if invited. But teachers sometimes shy away from performing to pupils. This is regrettable, for pupils love to hear their teachers playing. Pupils do not compare their teachers' performance against those of renowned virtuosi: they are often impressed by the most modest performances. A primary teacher learning the piano from scratch told me of the encouragement from her class as she progressed, over some weeks, from a tentative rendition of the melody of a nursery rhyme to a version using both hands!

I once attended a lesson in which a trainee teacher used part of a Debussy piano prelude—*La Cathédrale Engloutie*—as an illustration of loud/soft contrast. He knew the piece so well because he had learnt it as a pianist, but elected to use a recording as he was feeling a little rusty. The pupils listened quietly, and joined in a discussion readily. After a while, the trainee teacher wanted to replay a portion of the music to make a particular point. Rather than hunt round the recording, he went to the piano and played the part he wanted. It was only about ten chords, but the pupils lit up, and applauded. This trainee teacher instantly gained a clearer understanding of the greater immediacy to pupils of live performance.

When live music is not available, how might recorded music be chosen? Sometimes, teachers wish to tie listening to some other activity. Perhaps the pupils are to use the music as a stimulus for dance. Or perhaps it is to be related to work within a cross-curriculum topic. Where can one look for suggestions? Your own memory is the best resource available. If you want a piece of music that will stimulate the pupils to dance using short darting movements, then think of a piece that would inspire you to dance with short darting movements. Choosing a piece in this way means that the piece will be relevant to you, so you will, if necessary, be able to explain to the pupils how you wish them to respond to it. Whatever music you choose, you may find that the pupils' initial response differs from your own. This is simply because composers rarely write with the explicit purpose of implying a particular type of movement.

Published listening lists are often a great disappointment. In those for topics, pieces are often classified simply by the words in the title. Under the topic *Fire*, for instance, you may find Handel's *Fireworks Music*, Stravinsky's *Firebird Suite*, and the 'Ritual Fire Dance' from Falla's ballet *El Amor Brujo*. These pieces may, or may not, have anything to do with the aspect of fire that you are trying to depict. Handel's *Fireworks Music*, for instance, is ceremonial music intended to accompany a fireworks display: the depiction of fire was not Handel's main motive. Even if you happen to want some music to stimulate pupils to compose some ceremonial music to accompany a fireworks display, there is no guarantee that Handel's piece will do this successfully. I doubt Handel would have measured the lasting success of his music by your pupils' ability to guess 'fireworks display' when listening to the piece for the first time more than 250 years later.

Knowing about a composer's stimulus can, of course, inform the ways in which we listen to a piece. Penderecki's *Threnody to the Victims of Hiroshima* takes on a whole new level of terror once one becomes aware of the subject matter. And the fact that a piece was stimulated by the idea of *Spring*, for instance, can be interesting and useful to pupils who have just composed a piece using a related stimulus. My point is that we should not let the supposed meaning of the music obscure the music itself.

In *An Experiment in Education*,[2] Sybil Marshall (Marshall 1963: 189) wrote of her pupils' response to the second movement of Beethoven's 'Pastoral' Symphony:

'That tune's a swan', said Beverley from the floor . . . I said, 'I don't think Beethoven wrote a swan into it, Bev.' She looked up at me with eyebrows raised nearly to her hairline. 'How *do* you know?' she said.

Limiting our thoughts about a piece of music to some known stimulus can limit the listening itself.

Spotting sound effects can be as distracting as searching for more abstract images. A child attending an orchestral concert prepared himself for Richard Strauss's *Don Quixote* by reading the programme note. Clearly, this was going to be an action-packed performance. First he would hear Don Quixote tilting at windmills under the impression that they were giants, then there would be some sheep, and so on. In the event, he missed the windmills effect, mistook the sheep effect for creaking windmills, and then spent the rest of the performance waiting for the sheep.

Orchestral effects such as sheep impressions are rarely effective in any absolute sense. Their effect is relative to the sorts of sounds that orchestras usually make. If the pupils are not familiar with these, why should they recognize the sheep? And even if they do, why should they be excited, particularly if they are in a rural school, and there are some authentic sheep outside the window.

It is possible, and valid, to respond to music in some way that is outside the composer's intentions. Indeed, it is possible to respond to a piece without knowing what the composer's intentions are. Music chosen to support a topic need

---

[2] Sybil Marshall writes of a bygone age, but this is one of the most inspirational books that I have ever read. She was headteacher of a tiny village school, and used music, and the arts more generally, to motivate pupils who were, in some cases, reluctant learners.

not have any explicit relationship with the topic title. Where there is some relationship, the responsibility for relevance lies with the teacher, not the composer. We cannot hold Saint-Saëns responsible if listening to 'The Elephant' from his *Carnival of the Animals* leaves pupils wanting to talk about pet goldfish.

As with dance, the best source of suitable music for topics is your memory. If you are working within a topic of Growth, for instance, think of a piece you know that grows. I might choose Pachelbel's *Canon* (see p. 132). You might choose Ravel's *Bolero*, or something I have not heard of. Fine. The point is that, individually, we have taken responsibility for relevance.

What if you do not know much music? Clearly, nobody knows more than a very small proportion of all the music that could be played in a primary school. But everyone can develop a personal repertoire of listening material. You could approach this in much the same way as reading round a subject. Start from what you know and like, and work outwards, using CD notes, books, or shelves in audio shops as a guide. You may feel that there are whole fields of music about which you know nothing. Perhaps you know no popular music. Perhaps you know no orchestral music, or no Indian music. Here, it is perhaps easiest to find someone who is interested in the field, and ask them to suggest three or four pieces as a starting point. But do not feel that you need to be an expert in every field; no one can be. Pupils benefit from coming across teachers who have different special interests, as well as a willingness to grapple with the unknown.

An environment for listening

A recorded performance is, at best, an approximation to live music. And a classroom is not an authentic environment for listening. We cannot expect pupils to listen to a recorded performance in a classroom with the same enthusiasm or concentration as they would give to the same music played live at an appropriate venue. But recorded music does have one significant advantage over live music: pupils can listen to the same performance again and again, learning from successive listenings. And there are various steps we can take to produce a classroom environment that is conducive to listening.

1. We can choose a good-quality recording. A poor disk recording of a piece may help us to re-create a first-class performance we have attended; pupils hearing the piece for the first time will just hear the hiss and scratches.

2. We can choose an extract of an appropriate length. It is better to leave pupils wanting more, than bored.

3. We can prepare the extract well. Use of a temporary audio recording that fades in and out eliminates the disjointed listening experiences that arise when several shots at finding the right place are made.

4. We can choose a suitable quiet, comfortable, environment for listening.

5. We can present music positively. Pupils who anticipate that they are to hear something of value are more likely to give it their full attention. If the teacher shows no respect for the music by admitting a view that it is worthless, presenting it carelessly, or talking during it, why should the pupils bother with it? (The prize for the most negative presentation possible must go to a teacher reputed to play organ music to his class as a punishment.)

Purposeful listening

Should pupils be asked to listen, or asked to listen for something in particular? There is room in the primary school for both approaches. Ultimately, we want pupils to learn to listen on their own, but we can guide them as they learn.

Listening can be purposeful because the music is to be used as a stimulus for another activity, or because you have asked the pupils to listen with some particular features in mind. You might wish to check that the pupils have understood some particular concept, or to find out more about their perception of the music. You might wish to know if the pupils can disentangle a well-known tune embedded in the music, or whether they recognize any of the instruments being played. It is difficult for us, with adult ears, to predict how difficult pupils may find these tasks. If we find it easy to distinguish a solo oboe sound from a solo clarinet sound, for instance, it is because we have spent a great deal of time listening to the two instruments. Pupils have rarely had the same opportunity. Spotting individual instruments when they are being played as part of an ensemble is even more difficult. Every instrument sound is made up of a series of harmonics at different frequencies. Just think of the complexity of the situation that you are asking the ear to unravel. There are so many ways of listening to the same piece of music. By all means encourage pupils to recognize the structures you perceive. But beware of assuming that a child who does not hear what you hear perceives nothing of value.

Listening throughout music

This chapter is preceded by one on composing and another on performing. As we have moved through the sequence

composing → performing → listening

the chapters have become progressively shorter. Does this mean that the sequence describes a hierarchy, with listening being the least important activity? Not at all. This chapter is concerned with only a narrow range of listening activities: those in which the listener is neither performer nor composer. Listening is a thread that runs throughout composing and performing. And because of the interdependence of composing, performing, and listening, it makes little sense to talk about their *relative* importance.

But what do we mean by interdependence? Is use of the term just a pompous mode of noting the truism that composers and performers listen as they go about their business? Or is there more to it? To take the extremes of the sequence as an example, does experience in composing develop one's ability in listening to music composed and performed by others?

Some years ago (Mills 1989a), I carried out an investigation of pupils' development as listeners during immersion in composing. I visited a school before and after an intensive five-week programme of composing, and, on each occasion, asked the pupils to write down what they had noticed whilst listening to a particular piece of music: 'Mars' from Holst's *The Planets*. In almost every case, the quantity and quality of the second attempts were markedly increased. In particular, many pupils had stopped writing blow-by-blow accounts, and started to note the ways in which rhythm, mood, or orchestration developed throughout the piece. As the pupils had not listened to 'Mars' in school between my visits, and were not expecting me to ask them to repeat the exercise, it seemed that the improvement was due to the experience of composing. This is some limited, but encouraging, evidence of the interdependence of composing and listening. It suggests that the listening that takes place during composition can be at least as deep as that when the focus is listening alone. In an integrated and coherent music education in which pupils compose, perform, and listen, the boundaries between musical processes disappear. When pupils compose, for instance, they cannot help but learn as performers and listeners, as well as composers. That is what the interdependence of composing, performing, and listening is about.

PART II

DEVELOPING A FRAMEWORK

Part I has been concerned with musical activity which is fun and for all. Where development and progress have been mentioned at all, they have been short-term concerns. How could we develop the pupils' response to a particular activity? Given that the pupils have responded in a particular way, what might we say to them, or suggest they do next?

In music, as in any other subject, short-term consideration of development and progression is a necessary condition of effective teaching. But it is not sufficient. Part II is intended to help teachers work from first principles towards a framework for primary music that fits their particular circumstances. We start to address some issues relevant to the development of music within a primary curriculum to promote sustained, long-term progression and development. How do pupils develop in music? What might a music curriculum look like? How does the music curriculum relate to the whole primary curriculum?

In Chapter 6 I approach the matter of musical development by looking at some examples of research and enquiry in music education. There are, of course, many ways of making progress in music. But what can the results of research—including the sort that takes place far away from classrooms—tell us about the development of primary pupils as musicians?

In Chapter 7 I turn to the music curriculum. What are its aims? Who are we teaching? What music are we presenting, and why? I propose the idea of an entitlement curriculum intended to promote the musical development of all pupils without preference. How can we plan teaching without constraining pupils' musical development? How can we make sure that we are also meeting the requirements that are placed on us from outside our school such as, in England, the National Curriculum? How can what we found out in Chapter 6 inform our planning? We start with the planning of individual lessons, and then move towards more long-term endeavours.

As primary teachers we tend to speak of subjects, and subject learning, less than secondary teachers. We speak more of curriculum, and often of cross-curriculum learning. How does music fit in with this? We know that there are primary schools in which music occurs only as discrete subject study. What opportunities are being missed? In Chapter 8, I look at this from three oblique perspectives. First, I consider the role and organization of music within cross-curriculum topic work. Second, I look at some of the music that lies within a non-arts subject: science. Finally, I consider one application of music as a learning medium: the development of language.

Lastly, in Chapter 9, I start to look beyond the common music curriculum and beyond the classroom. In the past, school music has sometimes been a piecemeal operation centring on those pupils who seem particularly able as musicians. This form of organization is incompatible with the notion of an entitlement curriculum for all pupils (Chapter 7). I suggest ways in which school music can centre on the music education of all pupils whilst still offering optional opportunities for the further development of particular skills and interests.

Chapter 6

Musical development during the primary years

Musical development before starting school

How do pupils develop as musicians in the primary years? What can you expect of a 7-year-old composer? Is a 9-year-old ready to learn the violin? By what age should pupils be able to read music? Are there some musical activities that 6-year-olds do better than 11-year-olds?

Although psychological theories of learning could help us shed light on some of these questions, they would not be enough to enable us to find any answers. The questions are about musical behaviour, which is dependent on learning; none of them can be answered effectively without reference to the music curriculum that the pupils have been following. Just what can be expected of a 7-year-old composer depends on what opportunities for composing that child has already received, for instance. And because of the vast variation in the musical experience of pupils when they enter school, and the equally wide experience of music that they receive on arrival at school, none of these questions is currently answerable in any generalizable sense.

In *Music in the School* (Mills 2005: 163) I wrote of Amy, and her younger brother Tom, and their entry to music education when they were a few days old. (In a sense, Amy and Tom had already received 9 months of music education when they were born, but I am choosing to start the clock with their births.) Here is my first note on Amy (Mills 2005: 163–7):

Amy is ten days old. Her father lays her across his lap as he improvises at the piano. The harmonies are rich; the timbres are full; the mood is reflective—but the music is neither gentle nor spare. Amy turns her head towards the piano, remaining motionless until her father stops playing more than five minutes later. We do not know the shape of Amy's thoughts. But her attention to the music—its sounds, vibrations and the movement of her father's hands—which she is perhaps sensing through her ears, eyes and throughout the 'piano-side' of her body, remains rapt.

I continued:

What is happening here? Is Amy displaying signs of musical precocity? Is she going to become a great musician? Perhaps she is, perhaps she isn't. Another way of looking at the above is simply that Amy is:

- receiving some music provision
- responding to it
- lucky enough to have at least one adult observer who notices her response, values it, and who is in a position to give her some further musical provision.

In Amy's case, the musical provision that she received routinely included lots of singing with her parents and their friends, and the chance to 'play around' on piano and other instruments, or listen to her parents playing, on almost any occasion that she wished. It is possible that any child would respond positively, just like Amy, to such provision.

But this was not the end of the story:

Amy, [now] age 34 months, has a brother, Tom, age 5 days. When he cries, she tries to calm him through singing. She chooses songs from her repertoire that she feels will soothe him—such as a slowed down version of *Twinkle, Twinkle Little Star*, and sings to Tom in a special *sotto voce* voice.

I continue:

In National Curriculum terms, Amy is doing pretty well for a child under the age of 3. Through matching the mood of her music to an effect that she intends, and through showing the vocal command needed to do this consistently, she is well into the 'level 2' that is expected of children aged 7. That she has decided to do this for herself is interesting. Children can show their capabilities more clearly when they have the opportunity to act spontaneously, and for real. Had Amy been asked in a classroom situation to choose a song and sing it so as to make it suitable for a lullaby, she might have found this much harder. Amy might find it difficult, just yet, to explain in words what she is doing and why, but this does not diminish the fact that she knows what she is doing, because she does it.

What is the effect of Amy's intervention on Tom? In those early days, Tom tended to cry because he needed to, and so Amy's singing rarely had the intended effect of quietening him, much to her disappointment. However, within a few weeks, Tom is showing that he is developing sensitivity to singing: Tom, aged three months, gave his mother his full attention as she sang their family song, which is based on the opening of *Bobby Shafto*:

Mum, Mum, Mum, Mum, Mum, Mum, Mummy
Dad, Dad, Dad, Dad, Dad, Dad, Daddy
Tom, Tom, Tom, Tom, Tom, Tom, Tommy
Amy, Amy, Amy, Amy, Amy.

As she began to repeat the song, he started to join in with short phrases of gurgling. For two captivating 'Dads' he gurgled the same pitch as his mother sang. Half way through the third line all this effort became a bit much for him, and he fell silent. But he still gave his mother, and her singing, his full attention.

While it is impossible to check this out directly with Tom just yet, given his age, his parents, at least, think that he has got the idea about singing. And the sheer fact that he is responding makes it more likely that his parents will carry on singing to him in future. If Tom has not, contrary to impressions, got the hang of singing yet, it is difficult to see how he can avoid getting it in due course.

Amy's singing, on the other hand, is now going through a phase that one kindly might describe as 'interesting'. She is just 3:

On being invited by her father to record her singing on the computer, Amy decided on *Twinkle, Twinkle, Little Star*. She chose her own starting note. Perhaps it was a bit high. But she stuck in there, exercising her voice more thoroughly than had she started on a note chosen for her, and perhaps learning through experience that a lower note next time might be easier. Amy finds the 'st' of 'star' difficult to say, and so she stops after 'little' to take a breath, and gives a good loud 'star' which disrupts the phrase. Amy chose a tempo that was too slow for her to sustain, and she speeded up a bit.

Play Amy's 'performance' to an examiner, and the chances are that it would not get a good mark. Put on a backing track in a key and at a tempo that she can manage comfortably, and she would probably get much better 'marks'. But wouldn't it be sad if Amy never had the chance to work things out for herself? Amy's rendition of *Twinkle Twinkle* was 'work in progress'—'performing' rather than 'performance'. Amy is busy learning through play—with songs as well as almost everything else that comes her way—and an important part of learning is that of setting herself challenges which do not always quite come off.

There was time for another recording:

Supercalifragilisticexpialidocious, from *Mary Poppins*, which Amy sang after finishing *Twinkle Twinkle*, was even more obviously full of play.[1] The relish with which Amy worked her way round the difficult words of the first two and a half lines before collapsing into silence, and then a brief giggle, as the word 'precocious' eluded her was almost tangible. These were not the giggles of a child who was trying to please adults by being 'cute', but of a child who, mercifully, saw the funny side of having just made a bit of a mess of a recording. Being allowed to make mistakes is an important part of learning to be a great success. Amy is using singing to play with language, play with her voice, play with her memory. And when things go wrong it is still all fun. She is engaging with the raw materials of music, and learning continually. (Mills 2005: 163–7)

---

[1] For more on the role of play in musical development, see e.g. Marsh and Young 2006.

A notable feature of Amy's learning in music, at this stage, is its freedom. She is learning through play. Open-ended voluntary tasks give her the opportunity to show what she can do, and she frequently chooses to show that she can do a great deal. This enthusiasm for open-ended learning in music continues throughout the primary years, provided that it is not stifled by teaching of a more arid kind. This is good news for teachers who may be lacking in their confidence to teach music. Offer pupils the opportunity to complete an open-ended task in music, and they will show you, through their response(s), several worthwhile offers that you could make to them next.

Sandra Trehub (Trehub 2006: 44) has written:

In the case of very young children, music educators and parents should consider whether the expected benefits of training—more rapid achievement of some musical milestones—involve any hidden costs. Perhaps the greatest challenge for early music educators is to sustain the joys of music and the musical creativity that are so clearly evident in the months or years that precede formal instruction.

I observed a nursery class where five children had chosen to experiment with a range of classroom percussion instruments that were laid out on a table. The children had been there for at least half an hour. Some of the time they talked to each other. But they mainly worked individually trying out instruments, and modifying the ways that they played them to get exactly the sound that they wanted, and then showing their friends what they had done. They were engrossed in sound. A teaching assistant joined them and, without listening to what they had done previously, 'organized' them to play exactly the same simple rhythm at the same time—without regard to the timbre of the instruments, or their natural duration. The children cooperated while the teaching assistant was present, but left as soon as she did. The spell had been broken.

This teaching assistant did not make a positive contribution to these children's education. It would have been better had she done nothing, and just left the children to manage their own learning.

Several researchers have written on the 'natural' musicianship of pre-school children—all pre-school children. Rosie Burt (2007) has shown that young children assign emotions to music, in ways that are consistent with their peers. Margaret Barrett (2002a; 2002b), Esther Mang (2001), and Bertil Sundin (1998) have focused on young children's compositions. Patricia Campbell (1998) considers the many ways in which children use music in their everyday lives.

Primary teachers need not worry about needing to 'introduce' their first class to music. They need only create an environment in which children show what they can already do, and help them to steer their progress as they move through school.

Musical development at school

Before turning to the main focus of this chapter—the musical development of pupils at school—I offer a few thoughts on the musical development of teachers.

It has become a cliché to answer the question 'what subject(s) do you teach?' with the statement 'I teach children'. However this cliché remains useful to me, as it fits the aims of this book. We teach music in school so as to promote the development of pupils in, and through, music. We don't teach music in schools for the good of the subject. There are many ways in which pupils can develop in music through doing music at school. There is no need to use the, sometimes flamboyant, skills of music graduates to further progress in music lessons, provided that pupils are moving forward as musicians. There is no need for anyone in a primary school—teacher or pupil—to read a dot of staff notation, or play a single piano note, or recognize Stravinsky's *The Rite of Spring*, or Wagner's *Götterdämmerung*, from a recording. Indeed, there is no need for them to have even heard of either of these pieces.

Primary teachers can, of course, improve their skills. As part of a project on music, mathematics, and science that I carried out with colleagues at the University of Exeter, I tested trainee primary teachers there in music at the start and end of their training year, and found that their skills had improved substantially. This was not just the result of the small amount of music teaching that the trainees received as part of their course at the university. Like trainees everywhere, those at Exeter used their initiative to raise their skills:

Music lessons took place also at other times. [Students were to be seen teaching each other] in the common room, at the bus stop, and in school. Several students bought guitars or recorders and practised at home, and students who were parents enlisted the help of their offspring when they ran into difficulties with music reading. But even so, the gains made illustrate the capacity of well motivated students, equipped with the learning skills of the graduate, to learn far more within a given time than might, to a reasonable person, seem possible. (Mills 1995/6: 126)

The progress that the Exeter trainees made in mathematics and science was less impressive than that in music. Indeed, the test marks of primary trainees in mathematics and science deteriorated during the course (Bennett and Carré 1993). The enthusiasm that the same trainees had shown for developing skills in music was matched by that of primary trainees who I had taught a few years earlier, at Westminster College in Oxford. The trainees there wanted to teach music in primary school, but many thought that they did not have the skills needed to do this. On circulating some short questionnaires (Mills 1989b: 125–38), I learnt that 30 per cent of trainees felt least confident about teaching music, of the eight subjects that they were then expected to teach.

(The second most worrying subject was religious education (23 per cent).) Many of the trainees thought that they needed to be able to play recorder and read staff notation. They didn't actually need either of these skills, but not having them impaired their confidence, and risked impeding their progress as a teacher. I selected[2] the 25 per cent of trainees who agreed with the statement 'music reading is a complete mystery to me' to be withdrawn for a few minutes of their regular music class for a group session of recorder playing. We had a lot of fun in these recorder sessions. It was telling that trainees, when first summoned to the music room to work in this 'selected group', assumed that they had been chosen by mistake, so used were they to special provision in music flowing to those who are thought to be more able. But as soon as they saw that the group contained some reprobates more likely to be found in the local hostelry than at a recital of early music, they relaxed, and started to enjoy themselves. By the end of the first brief lesson they were playing cheerful two note melodies with backing tracks. After six such lessons, they performed to the rest of their year group. When I discovered, at the end of the year, that a small number of trainees had not taught any music in school 'because their school would not let them'—an unlikely story!—none of my special recorder group were numbered among them.

It is sometimes said that pupils need to learn some specific music skills when they are still very young. The examples of learning to read written music (staff notation), or learning to play some instruments, including violin, are often given. In fact, this is not the case, and teaching pupils these skills too early may damage their musical development. Pupils who learn to read music can forget how to play without it. Pupils who take violin lessons, for example, may not enjoy them, and 'give up' completely. Or they may even be told to give up by an unsympathetic instrumental teacher who has not spotted that a child's lack of formal progress is the teacher's, rather than the pupil's 'fault'. And does it actually matter whether pupils look to be destined for a successful career in solo violin, provided that they are making progress at their own speed, enjoy their work, attend scrupulously, and so forth? We don't teach pupils mathematics, for example, because they seem to be destined to gain a

---

2 The other options available to trainees were: 'I can work out the names of any notes in treble clef' (60 per cent); 'I know at least five notes on the recorder and their position in treble clef' (50 per cent); 'I can read bass clef fluently' (30 per cent); 'I can work out the timing of simple rhythms from their notation' (60 per cent); 'If I am given the music for a song, I can always work out what the melody sounds like' (30 per cent). Trainees also answered questions about their confidence as music teachers, relative to their confidence in other subjects; what they would do in their first music lesson with a new class; and listed activities that they were worried about leading.

Fields Medal. While many famous classical musicians did start learning when they were very young, this may have been because they wanted to, rather than needed to. A student studying at the Royal College of Music, in London, with a view to becoming a professional musician, told me how he had been 'sacked' by his piano teacher for finding it difficult to play with both hands together when he was very young. He took up another instrument in his teens, and is now doing very well. Harald Jørgensen (2001), who works at the Royal College of Music in Oslo, has found that much of the instrumental teaching that young people receive does not help them to make progress faster than their peers who learn music solely in class. In 1997 (Mills 1997a) I drew upon data from the national inspection of all primary schools in England and showed that, on average, primary class teachers teach music more effectively to their class than do 'specialist' teachers from another class, or outside school. There are exceptions of course—visiting specialists who teach well, and class teachers who don't—but the overall pattern is not this.

The main musical challenge for primary teachers is that of allowing primary pupils to build upon the musical experience that they brought with them to school, and will continue to develop during their time away from school, for example at home, or when they hear music being played in the street.

So, how do primary pupils make progress in music? Up to now in this chapter, I have written mainly of the progress that pupils make naturally, through being a member of society. But we also have further requirements that are made of us, not least that of following the National Curriculum for music in England, if we work in a state school in England (DfEE and QCA 1999). In fact, as I have already hinted, the National Curriculum for music in England is not a notably difficult curriculum for teachers to provide as it is short, and seemingly premised on the notion that pupils have not done any music before they came to school, whereas many of them actually have a head start.

Other subjects may seem to have patterns of development sewn up. Looking at the Attainment Targets and Programmes of Study for science (DfEE and QCA 1999b)[3] in the National Curriculum, for instance, one has the impression of an agreed primary science curriculum which reflects both the order in which pupils learn science, and the ages by which pupils can usually learn particular pieces of science. There are a number of historical reasons why there is so much more consensus about the science curriculum. As many more pupils are

---

[3] Up to a few years ago, mathematics or English would have provided the best examples of this point. But the introduction, and then relaxation, of the literacy and numeracy strategies has left some lack of clarity about what is meant by the National Curriculum in these subjects. Hence this use of science as an example.

examined in science at the age of 16, there has been a clearer sense of purpose and direction in science throughout compulsory schooling. Because of the wide use of published science schemes, there has been more commonality in science teaching. These are not necessarily points of which to be proud. An inappropriate model of the 16-year-old scientist could generate an equally inappropriate top-down science curriculum. Faults in a common curriculum, such as poor sequencing or low targets, would take longer to recognize because of the lack of alternative examples. Innovation requires autonomy. But primary teachers have a shared experience of science teaching which they lack in music; in science there is more of a basis for talking about development.

In Chapter 7, we consider curriculum planning in music. Before this, we look at some research in musical development which could inform curriculum planning. This is not because ideas should always be tried and tested before they are incorporated into curriculum practice; curriculum development requires a curriculum for development. The point is that thinking about the implications of research can sometimes illuminate the process of curriculum planning, and save us going down some blind alleys.

My choice of research is highly selective, and far from comprehensive. Overviews of particular fields can be found elsewhere (e.g. Hargreaves 1986; Parncutt and MacPherson 2002). My purpose is to highlight a few varied studies which have produced potentially useful results, and to present each in sufficient detail for some of their implications for classroom music to become apparent. The studies chosen are drawn from publications that are available, and which contain other interesting and useful research. The reader whose appetite is whetted can use the references given as a basis for more extensive reading.

It is customary, when writing of research findings, to attribute them to the researcher who first found them. In a short book, such as this, it is not always possible to follow up with references to every researcher who has applied, or developed, the original idea. Hence the wide range in the dates of the research that is mentioned in this chapter, in particular.

Research and enquiry in musical development

Since the early years of the twentieth century, and particularly over the last fifty or so years, research in the field of music education has mushroomed.[4] Early

---

[4] The research has mushroomed within the English-speaking world, and also beyond it. For example, in 2007 I requested a bibliography of music education research in Brazil, and received a substantial list of papers that I would not otherwise have known about. My thanks to Sérgio Luiz Ferreira de Figueiredo for preparing this list, and for providing a synopsis of each paper in English.

research, such as that carried out by Carl Seashore at the beginning of this period, was in the tradition of psychometric testing, and took place under carefully controlled conditions. It explored research questions concerned with musical perception. What is the highest note that can be perceived? What is the smallest pitch interval that can be recognized? Do the answers to these two questions depend on age? Measurement often required the use of sophisticated apparatus, and sometimes took place in laboratories.

Research into perception continues to this day and has relevance to music education which is sometimes overlooked. But, alongside this, a tradition of exploring pupils' activity as musicians is developing. Here, the research questions are more directly related to composing, performing, listening, and classrooms. How do pupils develop as composers? In what circumstances do pupils learn to sing in tune? And so on.

These two research traditions are not necessarily in opposition. The results of investigations in one tradition sometimes inform the questions asked in the other. Indeed, some researchers have worked in both areas at various points of their career. But because the questions asked are so different, and because the relevance of the research to music education is of a different nature, I consider the two areas separately.

Children as perceivers

Research in aural perception can be concerned with any of the parameters of sound, such as pitch, loudness, or timbre. I shall focus on just one aspect of perception: pitch discrimination. This is the ability to assess that there is a difference in the pitch of two tones. Investigations of pitch discrimination have often explored how close in pitch tones must be before they are judged to be the same. They may also explore whether the direction of the pitch movement can be assessed accurately. Thus an individual having his or her pitch discrimination assessed might be asked to listen to two tones and say whether the second one is the same, higher, or lower. One's ability in pitch discrimination depends on the frequency range used. Very high and very low intervals are harder to discriminate. The investigations referred to below use a frequency range in which pupils find discrimination particularly easy: their vocal range.

Pupils' pitch discrimination has been investigated by many researchers. The pattern that has emerged is as follows:

1. Children can discriminate very small intervals
In 1893, J. A. Gilbert (Shuter-Dyson and Gabriel 1981) found that children aged 7 could, on average, assess the direction of some intervals as small as two-thirds of a semitone. In the early 1960s, Arnold Bentley (1966) found that they

could assess one-third of a semitone. In the early 1980s, I found (Mills 1988a) that the average 7-year-old could assess an interval as small as one-sixth of a semitone, that is, a 1 per cent difference in frequency. Thus several researchers have agreed that normal 7-year-olds can discriminate very small intervals. Quite how small does not matter for the purposes of this argument. The discrepancies between the three sets of findings are probably attributable to the differing quality of the recording and replay equipment available at the time; there is no reason to suppose that the children of the 1980s necessarily had pitch discrimination any finer than those of the 1890s.

Researchers of pitch discrimination have often reported the results of work with pupils aged at least 6 years. This is usually simply because younger children might have difficulty coping with the test situation, which often requires pupils to write their responses. There is no evidence that younger pupils do not perceive fine differences in pitch. Indeed, Bridger (1961) observed that some babies aged under five days notice pitch differences of about four semitones, and they may be able to perceive much smaller intervals. It is difficult to understand how pupils could acquire language, and particularly accent, without some pitch discrimination.

Sandra Trehub (Trehub 2006: 43–4) has recently reiterated this point when writing of the accuracy of children's singing before they even enter school:

From what we know about [babies'] and toddlers' perceptual and motor abilities, it is highly unlikely that preschoolers' production 'problems' have perceptual origins. Instead, limitations in motor control (e.g. producing the intended note) and self-monitoring (e.g. noticing pitch or timing deviations from a model) must be implicated. In general, such limitations are outgrown in the normal course of development, but progress is likely to be accelerated by training.

2. Children's discrimination improves with age

Bentley and Gilbert both wrote of marked improvement over the primary years and into the secondary years. I found that the average 11-year-old was able to assess the direction of an interval of about a 0.85 per cent difference in frequency. Thus the average 11-year-old ear competes with much scientific equipment for sensitivity.

3. In any age group, there is a considerable range of ability

This has been observed by many researchers. I found some children as young as 9 who could judge the direction of an interval as small as one-tenth of a semitone; that is, about a 0.6 per cent difference in frequency.

What is the use of these findings? Researchers (e.g. Seashore 1938, Bentley 1966, Mills 1988a) used the range of ability, coupled with the observation that successful performers tend to have superior discrimination, as a basis for devising musical ability tests that include tests of pitch discrimination. The generally fine discrimination of pupils was, if anything, a nuisance. It meant that tests had to include very small intervals if they were to differentiate between pupils. And very small intervals are difficult to record accurately.

But some other implications of the three points outlined above have more immediate relevance to class teachers.

1. Teaching the concept of pitch (up/down)

Pitch is one of the basic concepts of music. Understanding of pitch is part of the National Curriculum for primary pupils in many countries, including England and Wales. Yet many 7-year-olds do not understand it. We might suppose that a child who has yet to achieve this objective is unable to perceive the pitch differences we are presenting. Our reaction might be to present progressively larger pitch differences to pupils, in the hope of finding an interval wide enough for them to notice. But, as the research shows that the average 7-year-old can discriminate differences much smaller than those usually used in music, the child's problem may be labelling, not perception (see Crowther and Durkin 1982). 'Up' and 'down' are terms associated with spatial movement. Their application to a musical context may need explanation and illustration. Teachers often approach this through the association of musical movement with spatial movement. Pupils may be asked to sing up a scale as they walk up some steps. They may use a hand to draw the contour of the pitch of a melody that they are listening to or singing.

Many pupils learn the concept of pitch easily using these sorts of techniques. Where problems persist into the later primary years, a teacher may wish to test a child's pitch discrimination using a published test (e.g. Mills 1988a), although I would not particularly recommend doing this. In any case, it would be unwise to assume that a child who does not sing well in tune necessarily has any problem with discrimination (see p. 63).

One question remains. If pupils have problems with the labelling of pitch movement, how do they manage to do pitch discrimination tests? The answer is, I think, linked with the recorded instructions that pupils are given as part of the test. These seem to be sufficient to enable pupils to apply the concept throughout the test, even if the pupils do not remember it, or become able to apply it on other more musical occasions. Certainly, some pupils who do not seem to understand the concept in a musical context display it during the test. Of course, there may be other pupils who would benefit from even more comprehensive instructions.

2. Coping with musically able children

The considerable variation in pitch discrimination in any age group means that some pupils have finer pitch discrimination than some teachers. This means that tuning tasks that are difficult for teachers are not necessarily difficult for pupils. A teacher is not necessarily the best arbiter of what is, or is not, in tune. This has some immediate implications. When pupils assert that two seemingly identical notes are different, we need to take them seriously. A child who complains that a guitar that her teacher has just tuned is out of tune may be justified. If such pupils are suppressed by statements such as 'it will do' or 'there's nothing the matter with it', they may not bother to listen so closely in future. Rather, their ability can be employed to the teacher's advantage: the pupils can assist the teacher with tuning.

There are all sorts of musical activities in which teachers can find that some pupils are more able than they are. This happens to everyone, not just those who have not had much official musical experience. The most highly qualified music graduates still find pupils who play some instrument or other better than they do. We have to suppress a natural reaction to be threatened by this, and instead work out how to use some pupils' ability to promote the development of less fortunate pupils, and also ourselves.

3. Diagnosing children's musical problems

The masking of fine pitch discrimination by difficulty with verbal labelling shows the need to think carefully about the causes of pupils' musical problems. Does inability to echo a clapped rhythm indicate poor rhythmic memory, or some difficulty with motor coordination? Does failure to walk in time with a piece of music necessarily mean that a child cannot hear its regular pulse? Musical perception takes place inside the brain; we cannot tap directly into it. If we want to know whether someone is perceiving accurately or not, we have to ask them to sing, speak, write, or move, for instance, and then measure how well they do that. Any problem may result from difficulty with the singing, speaking, writing, or moving itself, rather than the perception.

In 1996 I wrote an article on my observations of pupils' transfer from primary to secondary school in music.[5] Some secondary teachers seriously underestimated their pupils' prior learning, for example:

The [secondary] teacher took a large suspended cymbal, and a soft beater. First, she hit the cymbal softly at the rim. Second, she hit the cymbal as hard as she dared. She asked the [11-year-old] pupils if they could tell her in what way the second sound differed from the first one. One pupil volunteered that the second sound was longer than the first sound. No, that was wrong. Another pupil ventured that the second sound was more metallic, and the first more wooden. No, that was wrong too. A third pupil suggested that the pitch of the second sound wavered, whereas that of the first sound was higher, and more constant in pitch. No, that was still not right. Eventually, a pupil

---

5 Mills 1996. Parts of this article were reprinted in Mills 2005.

pointed out that the second sound was louder than the first one. When she evaluated this lesson at the end of the day, the teacher wrote that most of the class had not grasped the concept *loud–soft*, and were consequently still working towards the achievement expected of [7-year-olds in the National Curriculum]. (Mills 1996: 10)

This example could have easily related to pitch, rather than dynamics. I call this approach to starting at secondary school 'back to basics'. At any age, it has the capacity to underestimate seriously pupils' achievement. In suggesting that the pupils did not understand *loud–soft*:

the teacher was not in real life any more. And, although she may not have spotted this at the time, she was receiving some of the potentially confusing information that can result from trying to test pupils' musical understanding by giving them tests about very specific aspects of music. There is no such thing as 'context-free' music. You cannot give pupils a test of their pitch discrimination, for example, without presenting them with tones that have duration, loudness, and timbre, and it is difficult to be certain that pupils have homed in on pitch, rather than the other features of the music that are inevitably present. Pitch, duration, loudness, and so forth, are sometimes referred to as the 'elements' of music, but I believe that this is misleading, as they cannot be separated from each other in the way of the scientific elements. (Mills 2005)

4. Setting expectations for children

The significant variation in pupils' discrimination is a reminder of the need to guard against setting expectations of pupils so low that they become unable to show us what they can do. Recognition of the dangers of underestimating pupils is crucial to the effectiveness of curriculum planning.

The implications I have drawn from this research are personal. I have made use of the researchers' findings according to my particular circumstances as a music teacher. Teachers in different situations may see other implications as more significant. The point is that research questions that seem not to address concerns central to music education can still yield answers that are both relevant and useful. In particular, investigation of a characteristic that is at best only a component of musical activity can have implications relevant to music education.

That said, there are many research questions that can be answered more effectively through investigation of real music-making by pupils. We now turn to a selection of these.

Children as musicians

In this section, I focus on three studies. Each is based on pupils' ordinary musical activity in classrooms; in two the pupils are composing, and in the third they are performing. In each case, I draw out some implications of relevance to teaching and curriculum planning. The emphasis here is mine, not the researchers'. The first study, an investigation of pupils' sequential development as composers, culminates in the proposition of a model of composing development which may also have wider applicability. The second, an investigation of pupils' development as song composers, serves also as a reminder of the danger of adherence to a simple model; development is inevitably multi-faceted, and not always apparently sequential. The third, an investigation of primary pupils' developing vocal accuracy, points to the fact that a music curriculum intended for one group of pupils may be inappropriate for others. The studies were carried out some years ago, but their implications are timeless.

Children's sequential development as composers

How do pupils develop as composers? If pupils were all to follow the same pattern in their development as composers, then life as a music teacher would be straightforward. Given that a child had produced a composition at some particular position in this pattern, we would know where she or he was destined to move next; our job would be simply to lead the child there. As we all know, no aspect of child development—or even human development—is like that. Every model of learning is the result of some generalization, and few individuals follow any so-called normal patterns of development literally for more than the briefest period. There are many curriculum activities in which we accept this. Although we discern general patterns of development in pupils' writing or painting, we learn to respond to the expressive and technical aspects of work that seems to be out of sequence. We adapt reading and mathematics schemes to suit pupils' individual needs by adding a book here, or missing out a section there. The idea of a sequential model of pupils' musical development may be attractive, but we cannot expect it to answer all our questions about response to pupils' music-making.

In 'The Sequence of Musical Development: A Study of Pupils' Composition' (Swanwick and Tillman 1986), Keith Swanwick and June Tillman described a spiral model of development represented by the helix shown in Fig. 7. The theoretical basis of the spiral arises from consideration of the psychological concepts of mastery, imitation, imaginative play, and metacognition, and draws on the work of writers including Robert Bunting (1977), Helmut Moog (1976), Jean Piaget (1951), and Malcolm Ross (1984). The empirical evidence for the spiral arises from observation of several hundred compositions by 48 pupils taught, at various stages, by June Tillman.

The figures at the right-hand side of the helix correspond to the approximate ages at which Swanwick and Tillman believe pupils pass through the turns. Although only the first three turns are likely to be seen in primary school, I shall, for the sake of completeness, summarize all four. Using the explanation

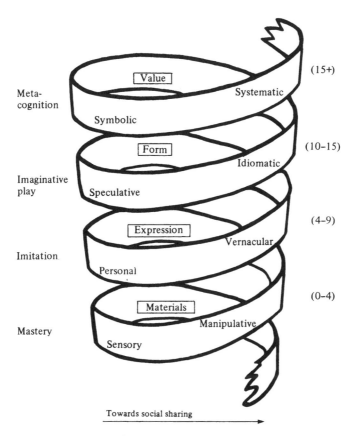

Fig. 7 The Swanwick/Tillman model of musical development.
Source: Swanwick and Tillman 1986: 331.

and examples provided by Tillman (1988), let us follow a fictional child, Julie, as she progresses, over ten years or so, from the sensory mode, and a concern with materials, through to the systematic mode, and a concern with value.

Turn 1: Materials

SENSORY MODE: As Julie explores the tone colour of instruments in a seemingly random manner, she seems to be asking the question: 'What sound does it make?' She is fascinated by the rattle of a tambourine, and the rasping sound of the scraper.

MANIPULATIVE MODE: Now Julie seems to want to organize the sound she makes. Sometimes she beats out a steady pulse. Some of the patterns that she chooses, such as a glide up and down a xylophone, seem influenced by instrument shape.

Turn 2: Expression

Julie's concern with materials continues. But two new modes develop:

PERSONAL MODE: Julie starts to show expressive character in her songs, and later in her instrumental compositions. The character is most clearly seen through changes in dynamics and speed. A song about the sun shining gets louder and faster until Julie 'almost shines herself'.

VERNACULAR MODE: As Julie starts to use repeated melodies and rhythmic patterns, her compositions become shorter and less apparently exploratory. Her composition appears more derivative.

Turn 3: Form

Again, two new modes develop:

SPECULATIVE: Julie starts to use contrast in her compositions. A repeated rhythm will suddenly change to give a feeling of surprise. Gradually, her use of contrast and surprise becomes more polished.

IDIOMATIC: Julie works within a particular musical idiom. This may be pop or jazz, or if she has taken piano lessons she may start to compose piano pieces in a style similar to those she has been learning.

Turn 4: Value

Now two final modes are added:

SYMBOLIC: Julie investigates a wider range of styles.

SYSTEMATIC: Julie develops a personal and distinctive style which draws on her work in various idioms, and which she may adapt for particular pieces.

The frame of reference of the spiral is the compositions of a group of pupils. Yet it seems also to explain some other musical behaviour. Swanwick (1988) applies it to the account of a teenage western classical musician at his first sitar recital. After some minutes of incomprehension, the teenager becomes impressed by the sounds themselves (Turn 1), then the shapes and colours they imply (Turn 2), before getting inside the structure to the extent that he becomes susceptible to surprise (Turn 3).

This is an experience that many of us have had as we start to listen to music of a type with which we are unfamiliar. To begin with, the music seems without shape, meaningless. We might wonder if the choice of notes and timing is arbitrary. Gradually, we find something that we can hold onto, even if we cannot explain what that is. Finally, we feel inside the idiom. We know what is arbitrary, and what is not. We accept the idiom on its own terms. This is the process that I likened to acquiring suitable spectacles in Chapter 5 (see pp. 77–8).

We have to be careful not to generalize too far from this. A model that works well in one restricted situation, and seems to make sense in another, is not necessarily true of all musical activity. We do not know, from the pieces of research that I have cited, if it applies to the work of other teachers on composing, or to performing, or to all forms of listening. Neither do we know the extent to which it makes sense to superimpose composing, performing, and listening spirals, for instance, and talk about a spiral of musical development.

Curriculum planning becomes less hassle-ridden when someone else has determined the aims of your curriculum. It can be tempting to cling to the spiral, to devise curricula intended solely to promote helical progression, and to assess pupils mainly—or possibly only—in terms of where, spirally speaking, they are. But the evidence for the validity of the spiral in all these contexts remains slender. And some potential areas of application would appear to require development as well as evidence. The use of a spiral mode for assessment is fraught with difficulty. If it is musical to revisit lower turns, for instance to absorb new musical experiences, then nobody can be assessed simply in terms of how high up the spiral he or she is.

It may still be helpful to think of the spiral as we try to make sense of pupils' music-making. But this should be critical thinking; we should be testing the spiral, not using it as a frame of reference. We should also be open to other ways of thinking about pupils' composing, performing, and listening. The responsibility for curriculum planning, teaching, and assessment must continue to rest with us. Being the best model around is not enough. If we don spiral-shaped blinkers, we may miss something even better.

Children's development as song composers

Coral Davies's article, 'Say it till a Song Comes' (1986; 1992), offers an approach to thinking about a particular field of children's composing: song. Davies reflects on a collection of more than 20 songs composed by pupils aged 3 to 13. She seems not to be searching for a pattern of development so much as for a way of responding to the composition itself. Thus her approach is more reminiscent of that of Loane's (1984) work with secondary pupils than that of Swanwick and Tillman. Most of the pupils concerned were not learning to compose in any sustained way. Often, they produced their songs so that they could sing them in a play. Usually, they wrote the words first, and then repeated them rhythmically until a song emerged, repeating the song until it became stable. Davies's approach is descriptive rather than experimental, and the reader is left to come to her or his own conclusions. The main points I take away from her work are as follows.

1. The role of adaptation within composing

Many of Davies's composers base their songs on material they already know. This leads Davies to argue that a rich musical experience helps with composing. Some adaptation was explicit. For instance, a 3-year-old based her song on *The Big Ship Sails through the Alley-Alley-O*. In other cases, the influence was better integrated. Adaptation seems to be taking place earlier than would be predicted from the Swanwick/Tillman spiral (Vernacular mode). It is possible that pupils are more likely to adapt if they are not presented with an alternative model through being taught composing.

2. The differing needs of children as composers

Davies argues the impossibility of producing a single progressive music curriculum that will suit all pupils. Some pupils arrive at school already making up songs, whilst others need a rich diet of musical experience as raw material, and possibly also specific help.

3. Differing ways of assessing progress in composing

Progress may be evident in many ways, including 'greater confidence in handling musical materials; an increase in melodic range, melodies which begin to open out rather than remain closed round the same few notes; a developing sense of shape and balance of phrases, or a more sustained, longer invention. It may be apparent in a more apt setting of words, use of more varied rhythm patterns, including syncopation, and a more imaginative turn of phrase in the words themselves' (Davies 1986: 288).

Davies's approach complements that of Swanwick and Tillman. She stresses the need for open-mindedness, thinking about composers and compositions on their own merits, and avoidance of prescriptive teaching. She comments on what is different, on what breaks the mould, whilst they look for what is common. The two approaches were developed in isolation; neither was a response to the other. They illustrate the differing ways in which researchers choose to make sense of what they see around them.

Singing in tune

Roger Buckton's (1988) study took place in New Zealand, but has implications of relevance to contemporary education in the UK. It consists of a survey of the singing accuracy of 49 classes of pupils aged approximately 6: 1,135 pupils in all. It is difficult for a researcher to assess the individual singing accuracy of pupils without making them self-conscious, and consequently distressed and likely to underachieve. Buckton's approach was to devise a technique for measuring the pupils' singing accuracy in a situation close to a usual classroom setting. Individual pupils were assessed whilst singing, with their class and teacher, songs that they knew well. Personal microphones were distributed to ten pupils at a time. As everyone sang a song together, two microphones were switched on, with the result that two of the pupils were recorded individually using the two channels of a stereo tape recorder. At the end of a verse, a new pair of microphones was switched on. By the end of five verses, all ten pupils had been recorded. Further songs were chosen until all the pupils in the class had been recorded.

Buckton graded the pupils' singing on a seven-point scale, which ran from

'7—sung consistently with a high level of vocal accuracy',

through

'5—occasionally vocally accurate, maintaining the general contour of the song, but singing incorrect intervals within that contour',

to

'2—spoken, or unclear as to whether the child was speaking or singing'

and

'1—invalid—no sound, indicating that the child was not singing, or a possible defect in recording.'

(Buckton 1988: 59)

Those pupils who were graded 1 (46 in all) were excluded from further analysis.

Analysis of the data shows, as usual, that the boys are less able singers than the girls. But, more interestingly, Buckton also analysed the interaction between ethnic background (as stated by the teacher) and singing grade. He found that the mean grade of Polynesian pupils exceeded that of European pupils, and that the difference in the mean singing grade of boys and girls was less marked amongst Polynesians. The results of comparing the mean singing grade of classes classified according to whether they were predominantly Polynesian, predominantly European, or mixed, were dramatic. When the 49 classes were arranged in descending order according to their mean singing grade—that is, starting with the class with the highest mean singing grade—the six predominantly Polynesian classes took first, second, fifth, ninth, and seventeenth place. Only one of the 32 predominantly European classes appeared in the top nine.

Why is this? Were the Polynesian pupils receiving more systematic training in singing in tune in school? Quite the contrary. The more successful European classes *did* have systematic training. For instance, teachers provided pupils with opportunities to sing individually and kept records of their development. They took account of the need to find pupils' comfortable range, and develop confidence within this before working outwards. But Polynesian classes, though they sang a lot, did not have systematic training in singing in tune. Buckton came to the conclusion that his findings were the result of an integration between cultural and educational factors. Singing is an integral part of Polynesian culture. Pupils sing with their families and in church from an early age. Fathers sing as much as mothers, so singing is probably less associated with females than it is in European culture. Pupils of European ethnic background, on the other hand, often arrive at school with little background in singing. Consequently, the educational needs of the two groups differ. The European pupils often need systematic help, whereas the Polynesian pupils just need practice.

What are the implications of Buckton's study for music education in the UK? It provides evidence that systematic singing tuition can help pupils learn to sing in tune earlier. But it also suggests that the system used needs to reflect the cultural and musical background of the pupils concerned. There is no one way of teaching pupils to sing in tune, and methods imported from other situations may be of no help. We need to work out what pupils' problems are, and plan accordingly.

Generalizing from Buckton's investigation of singing, it would seem that matching of the task to the child is as important in music as in any other subject. We need a mixed-ability approach to music teaching. It is inappropriate to take some externally devised music scheme, apply it to all pupils, and hope for the best.

So how might we plan in music? This is the matter to which we now turn.

Chapter 7

Planning curriculum music

It's relatively easy to have a party. (Ken Robinson on the need to think beyond one-off projects when talking of an arts curriculum)
NCC/SCDC Arts in Schools Project Conference, Warwick, 1989

Curriculum planning takes place on a range of different levels. The curriculum may be intended for a class, a school, an LA, or even a nation. The time over which the plan is to be implemented can vary from less than five minutes to the eleven-year period of compulsory schooling.

All curriculum planning takes place within a context of curriculum policy. The context may be defined by a complex combination of influences including government educational legislation, the curriculum policies of schools and LAs, and the educational philosophies of individual teachers. No two teachers operate in precisely the same curriculum context: individual differences in educational philosophy result in teachers within the same school implementing their shared curriculum policy in differing ways. The freedom of teachers to interpret external policies ensures a personal investment in the effectiveness of teaching, and facilitates curriculum development. Everyone in teaching—student teachers, newly qualified teachers, and teaching assistants, as well as the most experienced headteacher, LA adviser, HM Inspector or government minister—has responsibility for some level of curriculum planning.

Part I of this book was about the facilitation of musical activity. Chapter 6 has provided a narrow window into pupils' musical development. How can we use what we know about doing and development to plan teaching? First there are some questions we must address:

♦ To what extent should we plan music?

♦ What is curriculum music for?

♦ What music should we teach?

♦ Who are we teaching?

To what extent should we plan music?

Should we plan it at all? Doesn't planning take away the magic? Shouldn't every lesson be an exciting one-off experience? We need to have the 'parties' to which Ken Robinson alluded. But parties can become rather dreary after a while, particularly if you go to them three times a week, and it's always the same old crowd, and the same loud music. A music curriculum consisting of just one-off initiatives lacks, by definition, any intentional progression. Pupils may have fun—for a while. But if they make progress, this is through chance rather than design. Thus some planning is essential.

We must take care not to go to the other extreme. There are all sorts of ways in which planning can become counter-productive. A step-by-step curriculum in which every possible pupil response and permissible teacher action is specified would be dangerously restrictive, and would reduce the teacher to the role of a mere silicon chip. A curriculum led by a series of objectives for pupils to accomplish can result in underachievement if the objectives are too easily attained. What we need is a curriculum structure which gives a sense of direction to teaching, without constraining pupils' progress. This is difficult to organize, particularly in a subject in which there has, perhaps, been little agreed sense of direction in the past. There are many areas—composition, for instance—in which we are only just beginning to understand what pupils can achieve. In this situation, it is so easy to make mistakes, like those of teachers who assume (see p. 96) that a child who does not label one note as higher than another cannot hear the quality of the difference between the two notes.

There are no perfect solutions. I propose to adopt a model in which the sense of direction is determined by the overall aim of pupils' development as musicians (composers/performers/listeners). Surely this is sufficiently broad for it not to be constraining? In order to achieve this sense of direction, we need to set out what we want pupils to achieve in the shorter term. I shall call plans for shorter-term achievement objectives, though they could be called goals or expectations. But evaluation of teaching, and pupils' learning, will not consist simply of ticking whether or not pupils have achieved objectives. We will continually be on the lookout for pupils demonstrating achievement beyond, or outside, what we have set for them. That way, we can adjust our current objectives, and set more informed ones for the future. Along the way, we will also find out more about what pupils are able to do.

What is curriculum music for?

In Chapter 1, I offered some guidelines for curriculum music. Music is active, for all, and fun. These provide some pointers about the shape curriculum music might take, but offer little insight into why we are teaching music in the first place. What do we believe curriculum music offers pupils? In answering this question, I have in mind education throughout schooling, not just the primary phase.

The role of music in the curriculum includes the development of both expression and aesthetic awareness. Through music, pupils learn more about their culture. Music does not hold a monopoly on any of this. Creativity, expression, aesthetic awareness, and understanding of culture are embedded in all other subjects as well. But music, as an art, 'offer[s] unparalleled opportunities for the development of imagination, sensitivity, inventiveness and delight—essential elements in a balanced curriculum' (Paynter 1982: p. xiii). This is not all there is to say about music. Music is a way of learning. Music brings you in touch with pattern and structure. It requires reflection and analysis. So, of course, does every other subject. But music does have something rather special to offer here. Whilst you reflect on, or analyse, a piece of music, you cannot hold it in your hand, or even see it, for music exists in time; it is held only in your memory. To analyse music, you have to be able to use your mind rather like the controls marked on a CD player: to record, play, replay, fast forward, even rewind. The same is true of language. But music differs from language in being non-verbal. Thus music requires processes of reflection and analysis which are at least a little different from those of other areas of experience. Music enriches pupils' repertoire of ways of making sense of their environment. It is a crucial part of the development of the brain.

Pupils will take different things away from our music curriculum. Because we are teaching music, I have set an overall curriculum aim of developing pupils as musicians. But for some pupils, the extra-musical benefits of music education may be just as important as the musical ones. We cannot measure the effectiveness of our music curriculum simply by counting the number of pupils who go to concerts, or become professional musicians. But other possible benefits of music education, such as the development of the brain, are harder to quantify.

What music should we teach?

In Chapter 5, I said that no music is out of bounds to the primary curriculum. In the past, the music heard in British schools was, almost exclusively, of a restricted—though none the less important—kind, which I shall call 'European high art'. I use this term to refer, subjectively, to the music of composers including Bach, Beethoven, Mozart, and Tchaikovsky, whose many shared characteristics include the following two. First, they composed individually for an audience consisting mainly of those of high socio-economic status. Second, they transmitted their musical ideas through the use of manuscript paper.

Once upon a time, the dominance of high art in British schools might have been appropriate, or at least justifiable. If music education is about bringing pupils into contact with the great music of their own culture, then perhaps it makes sense for teachers to play a lot of the music that they regard as great. Today, this is not good enough. First, in a multicultural society our culture is not just European. Second, a notion that high art is great and other forms of European music are not great is open to question. Third, the transmission of our cultural heritage, whatever we mean by this, is only one part of music education.

There are really two multicultural issues involved here. First, world music is made up of different musical cultures with origins that can be defined, in a loose sort of way, geographically. Thus we might talk about Indian music, Chinese music, or European music. Second, any of these musical cultures encompasses a spectrum of subcultures. In the case of European music, subcultures include pop, opera, and Scottish bagpipe music. This analysis does not bear much inspection. Indian music, for instance, has taken on a life of its own outside the Indian subcontinent, and pop music is not just a subculture of music in Europe. Fusion is endemic in much of the music-making in the UK. The point I am making is that multiculturalism in music is not just about including music that originated outside Europe, but is also about reflecting the different subcultures of European music. These two dimensions overlap in a number of ways. But, for simplicity, I shall consider them separately.

British schools, traditionally, were predominantly concerned with so-called classical music, rather than popular music. Much of the music that pupils listened to was written by high art composers, and most of the songs they sang were classical songs, or classical-style arrangements of former folk songs. Doubtless, there were teachers all over the country who drew on pop music, but, like the teachers who encouraged all pupils to compose, they were regarded as quirky eccentrics until comparatively recently. The matter of whether it was appropriate for school music to be so biased towards classical music only started to receive a substantial educational airing in the 1970s. *Pop Music in School* (Vulliamy and Lee 1976), was one of the first publications intended to publicize and promote the popular music taking place in schools. Hence, for many pupils, there was a huge gulf between the music they did in school, and the music they listened to at home. In some cases, the gulf was more imagined than real; it had become part of teenage folklore.

Early in the 1980s, I was regularly greeted at the school gate by a particular secondary pupil who always asked me if we were going to listen to 'Beethoven' again today. In fact, as she well knew, we had not listened to anything composed by Beethoven all year. 'Beethoven' had become, for her, a generic term encompassing all so-called classical music. Actually, we did not listen to much of that either. But, despite my attempts to use pop music intelligently in the classroom, this pupil still saw a yawning chasm between 'Beethoven', which she identified with school and me, and the New Wave which she enjoyed outside school. This pupil was not typical of her age group; her views on many aspects of school life were extreme. And I still had much to learn about the use of pop music in school. Other teachers have been much more successful in reducing the home/school divide in music. But, to dream for a moment, would it not be preferable for there to be no divide in the first place? It cannot be eradicated overnight. But an approach to primary music in which all forms of music and music-making are valued would be a step in the right direction.

There are social reasons for including extra-European music in primary school; in multicultural Britain, how could a music curriculum consisting only of music with European origins be justified? There are also musical reasons; there is much that all musicians can learn from participating in music from a range of cultures. Paynter (1982: p. xiii) wrote: 'In education, our task is to reveal the breadth of music's expressive possibilities, not to restrict them.' Swanwick (1988: 113) wrote of 'inter-cultural music education', in which a range of musical styles are introduced 'not as "examples" of other cultures, with all the stereotyping and labelling that goes with such an approach, but as objects and events carrying expressive meaning within a cohesive form'. I have learnt much about music, and myself as a musician, through playing gamelan a little. This 'orchestra' of Javanese or Balinese instruments is typically played without any written music. Through playing in some gamelan classes, each of them taught in a different way, I have found that I am less dependent on notation when I return to my violin, and so play it better, with much more awareness of the sound that I am making, and how this sound relates to that of my fellow musicians.

Whenever we participate in the music of one or more cultures to which we do not belong, we must consider the issue of authenticity. It would be wrong to pretend that we can make authentic Javanese gamelan music, for instance, on xylophones, metallophones, and glockenspiels. There are many steps we can take to make our participation more authentic. These range from engaging practising musicians, through acquiring better resources, to just finding out more about the music. But inability to generate authentic participation in a particular music does not mean that we should steer clear of it. Classrooms are not authentic places for any form of musical activity. Listening to the music of Mozart takes place authentically at a concert, or at home in comfort, in response to the wish of the listener to listen. Real popular musicians do not work in class-rooms, constrained by the school timetable. Yet it is still appropriate to listen to *Eine Kleine Nachtmusik* and to compose popular songs in school. What is important, I think, is that we are honest with ourselves, and with pupils, about when we are trying to make music authentically, and when we are not. And if we are trying to make the music of a culture to which some of our pupils belong, we can draw them into the authenticity debate, and learn from them.

Music exists outside its culture. Swanwick (1988: 112) has argued that 'It is discriminatory nonsense to say that we cannot understand something of, say, *oriental* music without understanding oriental culture, the oriental *mind*'. If we do not need, always, to be making or appraising the music authentically, what should we be doing with it? We should be listening to it, performing it, and perhaps using some of the ideas we learn from it in our composing. As part of this, we will also be talking about it. Inevitably, what we hear and what we like will be conditioned by what we already know. That is right; if every listening experience was a one-off, how could we talk about development in listening? But if we are to learn anything from music of an unfamiliar idiom, we have to make an effort to listen to it on its own terms, not just through the spectacles that we use for the music we know and love. There is no point in measuring a piece of Japanese classical music against the yardstick we usually use for brass band music. It is sometimes difficult to avoid doing this. We have, perhaps, to wait whilst we progress through the spiral experience reported by the teenager at his first Indian music concert (see p. 102). This may mean waiting for a long time before we speak at all. And it may also mean letting pupils listen on several occasions before we expect them to say anything.

Who are we teaching?

Music is for all. We need a music curriculum which is intended for all pupils, whatever their musical background, race, gender, or educational ability. This is really a matter of developing a mixed-ability approach within which pupils are viewed as individuals, not stereotypical representatives of some particular group.

There are huge variations in the extent and range of pupils' musical back-ground. It is well known that pupils from musically supportive backgrounds are more likely to become accomplished musicians. This will always be the case; these pupils have had more musical experience than anyone else. But it is nonsense to pretend that everyone else is doomed to failure, whatever that means. Buckton's research (see p. 104) offers an instance of planning that was effective because it reflected pupils' background. We need a mixed-ability approach which enables pupils with little musical background to develop a firm foundation from which they may grow. Simultaneously, it must broaden and deepen the musical experience of pupils with more extensive background. This is a challenging notion, particularly when we reflect on the range of initial musical experience which pupils in our multicultural society may have. But it is one which we have to keep in mind if our claims to a mixed-ability approach are to be more than just rhetoric.

The curriculum needs to be suited to pupils of any cultural or racial background. This needs three forms of action. First, it requires a welcoming response to pupils who have not been brought up within the musical culture of the majority in their class and who, consequently, are not familiar with the material used. Second, it needs acceptance of the musical culture of all class members within the model of world music that is being adopted. Third, it requires avoidance of racial stereotyping. There is no evidence of differences in the innate musical abilities, or predisposition towards music of racial groups. Research in this area has always been inconclusive. Where differences in musical behaviour have been observed it has always been possible to attribute these to factors of social background.[1] Thus individuals living in the UK deserve to be treated as members of a culturally and racially diverse society.

The music curriculum needs to be fair to both boys and girls. In the primary school, we often find more girls than boys participating in voluntary music activities, particularly choirs. We have already seen, in Chapter 4, that the lower number of boys who are able to sing in tune cannot be accounted for solely in terms of their slower physical development. In Chapter 6, we saw that one explanation for boys' poorer singing might be parental role models: fewer European men sing. If boys are to have a fair chance in music, we need to try to compensate for this in school. Because of the disproportionately high number of women teachers and teaching assistants in primary schools, there is no way that we can deluge boys with models of men singing. But we can take other steps. The first is to encourage male members of staff to sing whenever possible. The second is to avoid presenting an excessively feminine model of singing. This means avoiding songs with soppy words, and making sure that boys get just as much encouragement with their singing. Lastly, we may also be able to tackle this issue sideways. In schools where music is taught mainly by women and yet there are plenty of boys in the choir, singing is often not the only focus of the music curriculum. Sometimes there is a great deal of composing. Alternatively, there may be emphasis on instrumental performance. Boys

---

[1] For instance, Igaga and Versey (1978; 1977) compared the rhythmic abilities of Ugandan and English children.

participate in composing, and much instrumental performance, on equal terms with girls—without the handicap of negative parental role models or developmental lag. It seems as though the musical self-esteem that develops here transfers into singing. Thus we need a balanced music curriculum.

Our mixed-ability approach to music needs to encompass pupils with special educational needs (SEN). All pupils have the right to an appropriate music education. And music can assist with the language development of pupils with learning difficulties. This has led to the development of teaching programmes based on the parallel development of SEN pupils' cognitive, language, and music skills.

Why should music help with the development of language? Motivation may be a factor. But so might cerebral organization. Studies of the brain have suggested that activity concerned with language takes place in the left hemisphere, and that music activity takes place predominantly in the right hemisphere. There is, however, evidence that the activities of the two hemispheres can reinforce each other. Left-hemisphere stroke victims can sometimes be taught to redevelop the language centre of their brain through right-hemisphere activity such as the presentation of sung language. If a child's language centre is underdeveloped, this may be stimulated through the presentation of sung language. Naturally, this effect is not confined to SEN pupils. There are situations in which many individuals find it easier to recall language when it is embedded in songs.

There are two groups of pupils who may have some practical difficulties with music-making: those with physical disabilities, or with hearing impairment. Here, I refer very briefly to some of the implications of their involvement in mainstream music. Teachers who have physically disabled or hearing-impaired pupils in their classrooms will also want to take some specialist advice.

Pupils with physical disabilities may still be able to play some instruments; others may require adaptation. One-handed recorders have been developed, and electronic instruments offer the possibility of an exciting range of sound played in a variety of ways. Just occasionally, one can see practice which, though well intentioned, is not offering a disabled child the best opportunity to become a musician. I recall observing a boy in a mainstream class who had the use of only his left hand, and no prospect of gaining use of his right hand, being taught to play the recorder with a teaching assistant supplying his own right hand as necessary. The intention was for the boy to participate in music alongside his peers. This he did. I observed him—or rather both of them playing *London's Burning* with the rest of the class. The problem was that the boy was never going to be able to play *London's Burning*, or much else for that matter, without the teaching assistant. This school had a policy that all pupils played the recorder.

Perhaps this was why they seemed to take a sledgehammer to crack a nut. Surely, an electronic keyboard would have provided a more effective, and cheaper, solution to this boy's practical problem with performing?

In the past, hearing-impaired people have sometimes been written off as musicians. The reasons for this have often been simplistic: music is sound, and the sound reception of deaf people is limited, if not non-existent. In fact, there are many examples of successful musicians with hearing problems. Schumann suffered from tinnitus. Beethoven wrote some of his greatest works when totally deaf. Recently, deaf musicians, including some who have been deaf since birth, have been awarded music degrees, and become professional musicians.

This is not as illogical as it might at first seem, for two reasons. First, the majority of so-called deaf people have some residual hearing; technical aids can help them to make the most of this. Second, perception of music is not a simple matter of the transmission of music from an instrument through the air and our ears to our brain. The sensation we call music does not exist without the brain; it results from the conversion of sound waves to electrical impulses which the brain processes. Thus, even those with no hearing—probably less than 10 per cent of the so-called deaf population—may be able to perceive a vibration-induced sensation which is as real as music.

Hearing-impaired people typically do not have hearing loss that is uniform throughout the frequency range. Thus some parts of the frequency range may be heard perfectly, with others being imperceptible. This can produce an effect rather like listening through a hopelessly adjusted graphic equalizer. Sounds that hearing people regard as extraneous, such as the clatter of a harpsichord keyboard, can dominate the music. Devices similar to graphic equalizers can be used to correct this problem, at least partially. Natural amplification can also be helpful: for instance, a hearing-impaired person who lies on a sprung wooden floor and listens can report a more substantial sensation.

We have been considering music in the education of pupils with special educational needs. Apart from the reference to language development, we have focused on music for music's sake. This contrasts with music therapy, in which the aim is therapy, and the music is present simply as a means of communication between the therapist and client. In *Music Therapy in the Education Service* (APMT 1988: 5), music therapy was explained as follows:

The ability to appreciate and respond to music is an inborn quality in human beings. It is well known that this ability frequently remains unimpaired by handicap, injury or illness. People who have difficulty in understanding their environment, or whose verbal communication is an inadequate form of self-expression, may nevertheless be stimulated by music and respond to it. Music therapists seek through music to arouse and engage clients, and to help them towards realising their potential.

Despite the differing purposes of music therapy and music education, the activities which take place in the two fields have some similarities. Traditionally, qualification as a music therapist in the UK was open only to music graduates. However, recent initiatives in in-service training in some LAs and universities, for example, have enabled other teachers to gain further understanding of the therapeutic use of music, and to learn some therapeutic techniques.

Summary

When planning curriculum music, there are several questions which can be kept in mind:

◆ What am I hoping pupils will achieve from my teaching?

◆ Why do I want them to achieve this?

◆ Will pupils be able to show me that they can achieve more than I expect?

◆ Am I presenting a programme that offers breadth as well as depth?

◆ Is my planning suitable for everyone present?

These questions—and their answers—provide the context for planning. We now turn to the planning itself.

Planning a lesson

There are two main ways of planning music lessons, or indeed any lessons. You can ask 'What do I want the pupils to *do* today?' or 'What do I want the pupils to *achieve* today?' The first, activity-based, way of planning usually requires less thought. The teacher just reviews the available resources—songbooks and so on—and decides what to do, with due consideration to what the pupils have done before. The second, objectives-based, way of planning usually requires more cognitive effort. One has to think about purpose as well as activity. The benefits of this method include the potential for a lesson that contributes to the musical development of the pupils in some intentional way. There may be some situations in which the first sort of planning is adequate. Certainly, most of us have been driven to it occasionally through exhaustion or lack of time. But activity-based planning runs the risk of leading to entertainment, or perhaps occupation, rather than teaching; it is not our concern here.

So lesson planning consists of finding answers to five questions:

1. What have the pupils achieved already?

2. What do I want them to achieve in this lesson?

3. How will I go about enabling them to achieve this?

4. How shall I assess whether they have achieved this?

5. How shall I avoid limiting pupils' achievement to what I have set for them?

Curriculum planning in all subjects consists of the continual revisiting of these questions. A teacher uses them to set up a curriculum plan for an entire academic year, but returns to them at many points during this period, including every occasion on which she plans a lesson. This may lead to adjustment of the original plan. But here the focus is narrow: a single music lesson.

Question 1: What have the pupils achieved already?

If you do not know what skills, concepts, and knowledge pupils have already learnt, what guarantee have you that your teaching will help them to develop as listeners, performers or composers? And if you do not know where the pupils started from, how can you evaluate their learning?

How can we establish where pupils are as listeners, composers, and performers? We can do the following:

Consult records of their previous work

- What was the content of their previous experience?
- What was their response to this content?
- What concepts and skills have they been taught?
- What concepts and skills have they learnt?

And so on.

Question them

- Do they understand the concepts they were taught?
- What do they remember of their work?
- What do they think they learnt from it?
- What do they think they have not yet learnt?

And so on

Observe them during musical and other activity

- What musical skills do they display?
- What musical skills do they fail to display?
- What related social skills do they display?
- What attitudes do they display?
- What concepts are they applying?

And so on.

Exactly how you frame your questions will be influenced by the phraseology of the curriculum document within which you are working. Some teachers and teaching assistants in England may wish to start by using the Attainment Target for music use given by QCA in the current, 2000, version of the National Curriculum (DfEE and QCA 1999a). Others may prefer to draw upon commercial materials. A Devon teacher who had held onto his LA curriculum document, *Music-Lines* (Devon County Council 1988), might prefer to rely on this. In that case, he might ask whether his new class of 6-year-olds could 'Use the words *loud* and *quiet* appropriately when describing and selecting individual sounds?' A teacher in another LA implementing a school curriculum document might ask, 'Can they use a variety of beaters to make *loud* and *soft* sounds on a range of instruments?'

Question 2: What do I want the pupils to achieve?

When starting a new project, or working with a new class, your initial assessment will be wide. You will want to find out as much about the pupils as possible. When you come to form objectives for your teaching, you may need to cut down your field of activity considerably. It is just not possible to tackle all areas of composing, performing, and listening simultaneously. How you do the cutting down could be based on several considerations, for example:

- Long-term balance between listening, composing, and performing.
- The pupils' preferences.
- The need to respond to individual differences.
- The priorities expressed in your curriculum document.

Objectives state the purpose of teaching. Musical objectives are concerned with pupils' development as listeners, performers, or composers. A Devon infant teacher implementing Stage 4 of *Music-Lines* (Devon County Council 1988: 15) might set the following objective for a series of singing lessons: 'The pupils will be able to sing several songs roughly in tune with me.' When setting this objective, she need not specify the songs that the pupils will attempt to sing. The mastery of material, in this case a series of songs, simply provides the means of accomplishing her objective. Materials are chosen in response to question 3.

Question 3: How can I enable the pupils to achieve the objectives?

Once we know where pupils are, and have decided where we wish to take them next, we are free to determine the process and content that we will use to do this. In other words, we are ready to plan the lesson itself. Usually, we will wish to set the activities intended to achieve our objectives in the context of a lesson which gives pupils an opportunity to warm up, allows for development and consolidation of learning, maintains pupils' interest, and so on. This aspect of planning is, of course, not subject-specific.

There are always several ways in which a musical objective may be accomplished. Our choice of approach depends on many factors, not least the extent of our own musical expertise. Teachers with extensive formal music skills usually have more choice of approach, but rarely a greater chance of success. As examples of this point, I have chosen two of the objectives for 11-year-olds stated in *Music from 5 to 16*. Both of these examples are relevant also to the National Curriculum in England (DfEE and QCA 1999). In both cases, I suggest a range of approaches intended to move children towards accomplishing the objective.

Example 1

'To know from memory and be able to join in with songs for assembly.'

APPROACH 1   Teach Parry's *Jerusalem*, accompanying the pupils by playing Parry's very difficult piano part.

APPROACH 2   Teach Parry's *Jerusalem*, with the additional support of a visiting pianist.

APPROACH 3   Teach the pupils a song that you can accompany on the guitar.

APPROACH 4   Teach the pupils a song that needs no accompaniment.

Note

Music from 5 to 16 does not specify that pupils need to learn *Jerusalem*, or indeed any other named song. Pupils who have not learnt *Jerusalem* by the time they enter secondary school can hardly be said to be culturally deprived. If you think that *Jerusalem* is an appropriate song, and are able to play the piano part, or have a colleague able to help you out, then go ahead. Otherwise, choose a song that is within your capabilities as an accompanist, or which sounds better without an accompaniment. You will still be working towards the same objective; the pupils will not lose out.

Example 2

'Be able to recognise the various elements of music such as . . . chord . . .'

ALL APPROACHES   Start work on this objective by drawing pupils' attention to the differences between chords and notes played in isolation. First explain that a chord consists of two or more notes played simultaneously. Continue with one of the following approaches.

APPROACH 1　Play some random chords on the piano, or keyboard. It does not matter how strange they sound. Occasionally play single notes. Check that the pupils can hear when you are playing a single note, and when you are playing a chord.

- Give them some difficult examples, for example a chord consisting of two notes an octave apart.[2] Play some chords of two, three, or four notes, and ask the pupils how many notes they can hear. Demonstrate the correct answer by building up the chord note by note.

APPROACH 2　If you play guitar at all, use your guitar. Play the pupils some chords you know—perhaps D major[3] and E minor—and check that the pupils can distinguish these from single notes.

- If you are able to, play some octave chords as suggested above for the piano. Play some invented chords; again, it does not matter how strange they sound. If you are able to, demonstrate several major chords. Ask the pupils to distinguish between major and invented chords. Repeat for minor and invented chords. Finally, try major and minor chords.

APPROACH 3　Use an electronic keyboard, or synthesizer, that has chord buttons. Repeat Approach 2 using the chord facility to provide automatic chords. Play single notes.

- Play invented chords yourself on the keyboard.

Possible extension for teachers using any approach who are able to harmonize simple melodies by ear.

- Explain that the chord of C major consists of the notes C, E, and G in any order, and that the chord of G major consists of the notes G, B, and D in any order. Divide the pupils into five groups, one for each note, and organize the playing of the chords. Use the chords to accompany a simple melody, for example *Three Blind Mice.*

---

[2] Choose any note on the piano. Find the closest note to the immediate right or left which is at the same point in the pattern of black or white notes. These two notes will have the same letter-name. Play them together and you have an octave chord. It is generally agreed that an octave chord is relatively hard to distinguish from a single note.

[3] In guitar notation, the symbol D is used to denote the chord D major, the symbol G is used to denote the chord G major, and so on.

Note

All these approaches exceed the requirements of the Example 2 objective (from the points marked ◆). The objective does not, for example, specify discrimination between particular types of chords. Thus pupils can be offered the opportunity to work towards this objective by teachers who do not know how to work out which notes are in the chord of D major, for instance.[4] In fact, teachers who do not know the so-called rules of harmony often approach this objective more imaginatively. Cognoscenti can be inclined to restrict themselves to the official chord forms that they know, for example major and minor chords. This gives pupils a limited, and culturally biased, idea of the range of sounds encompassed by the term 'chord'.

These are just two examples of the ways in which teachers can take into consideration their own musical expertise when deciding how to facilitate pupils' accomplishment of curriculum objectives. This principle can be applied to all the objectives for primary music in most of the recent curriculum documents I have seen, and also to the National Curriculum. I repeat a point that I made earlier because I think it is so important: teachers with extensive formal expertise often have more options concerning the means they can use to accomplish curriculum objectives, but they do not hold a monopoly on successful curriculum implementation.

Question 4: How shall I assess whether the pupils have achieved the objectives?

Often, objectives can be turned into a question form. An objective: 'The pupils will learn to maintain a steady beat for a short while without help' is easily turned into the question 'Can the child maintain a steady beat for a short while without help?' This is not a very precise question. How steady is steady? How long is a short while? How much help will the child get in starting the beat, and what speed will the beat be? Within the present context—the setting of objectives for an individual lesson—I do not think this matters. We are not trying to set a national standard of steadiness. As the teacher makes assessments of the pupils' achievements, he or she will develop standards to suit that teacher's purpose. The teacher might be particularly interested in what *all* the pupils are able to do, and what, perhaps, only ten pupils can do. One teacher's standards may not be exactly the same as the teacher's in the next room, but then the assessment is not being made with the purpose of comparison between the two classes.

---

[4]   However, there is no great mystery to this. Such matters are best taught live, not through a book. Ask a friend or colleague for help.

The need to use seemingly woolly questions for assessment is even more apparent when the pupils have been involved in a more complex activity, perhaps composing. An objective for the pupils, 'To learn to use contrast within their compositions', for instance, may result in a question such as 'Can the pupils use contrast in their compositions?' How much contrast? What sort of contrast? Is the use of contrast to be well integrated, or is it all right for it to stick out like a sore thumb? Again, the teacher is not asking this question as part of a national survey of contrast within composition. The personal validity with which she or he applies the question is sufficient. And the teacher does not need to answer the question with a simple 'yes' or 'no'. Responses may include 'Yes, but the group's compositions have now become very disjointed' or 'I do not know. His piece started slow and ended fast, but I am not sure whether this was intentional or not. I think he says it was intentional just to please me.' In both these cases, the teacher's responses will help him or her to set future objectives. Thus the purpose of the assessment has been fulfilled. The teacher may choose to set more refined objectives which are more amenable to assessment in the future. There is no point in setting objectives that are any less clear than necessary. But hopefully this will never end up with the tail (assessment) wagging the dog (teaching). It is far better to have some slightly inexplicit questions that make sense to the teacher and deal with music as a holistic experience, than to set only clinical objectives which could be measured by a machine and have little to do with music.

Question 5: How shall I avoid limiting pupils' achievement to what I have set for them?

That we structure pupils' experience by teaching them at all reduces the directions in which they can develop. But we believe that by teaching pupils we open new doors to them which they would not have opened, or even located, for themselves. Thus the business of not constraining pupils' achievement is, in a sense, a damage-limitation exercise. But there are several constructive steps that we can take. First, we can keep our eyes and ears open. When observing pupils making music we need to notice the things they do that are outside the objectives we have set. We need to see and hear the child who may or may not be achieving an objective of 'composing short melodies on a tuned instrument' but who is showing an astonishing facility in playing a xylophone. 'What else did I notice?' can become a routine part of the evaluation of pupils' learning. Second, we can set open-ended assessment questions which enable pupils to show they can do more than we think. 'Can the child maintain a steady beat for a short while without help?' might enable a child to show she can do this at a variety of speeds including some slow ones which we might have thought were too difficult. Third, we can vary our styles and modes of teaching from time to time so that pupils have a variety of opportunities to show us what they can do that we have not asked for.

Planning on a larger scale

The previous section referred to short-term planning: just one lesson. It concerned a teacher planning for his or her own class, and working within the context of a curriculum scheme that is already defined. Now we move to consider planning on a larger scale: the production of a school music curriculum scheme. This will, of course, need to meet the requirements of a National Curriculum in any country that has one. However, the requirements of the National Curriculum for music in England were never extensive. Curriculum planners can start by drafting a curriculum that is musical, appropriately demanding, and fun, and then check this against the National Curriculum. They do not need to begin by working through all the individual points of the National Curriculum, and then adding them together into an enormous document. Thus teachers can develop a music curriculum that meets the musical needs of pupils, and exploits the differing musical strengths and interests of teachers within their school.

Devising a school curriculum document is rarely a matter of starting with a blank sheet. Usually, the school already has a music curriculum which will be developed. How might one go about this? Reflection on the current curriculum, its aims, its strengths and weaknesses, its coherence, what is missing, what is there that cannot be justified, and so on, can be a useful first stage which draws in everyone involved. This may result in agreement that the current curriculum plan needs little revision. Perhaps just a little fine tuning is needed to update the use being made of information technology or to strengthen progression within composing. Suppose, however, that it is agreed that a complete rethink is needed. What issues should be addressed? Many of the points considered in the section on lesson planning apply here but on a larger scale. In addition, the ways in which the curriculum can be adapted by teachers of differing musical experience may need to be spelt out. The 'programmes of study' for the National Curriculum, and non-statutory guidance from government bodies such as the QCA will be helpful in defining aims. Below are some further matters for consideration.

Finding a feasible approach to curriculum planning

There is no one ideal way of writing the curriculum for your school: there are millions of feasible ways, and you just have to find one of them. An approach different from yours may be better, or may just be different. John Paynter (1982) suggested two feasible approaches to thinking about the secondary-school music curriculum. The first is based on musical concepts, the second on the techniques and structures found in the music of professional composers. Both approaches involve pupils in composing, performing, and listening; only the focus differs. Either of these approaches could be applied, with suitable consideration of the development stage of the pupils, to the primary school.

Some LAs have recent curriculum documents that are available for schools to draw on, free of charge. When considering whether to purchase a commercial music scheme, it can be helpful to check that its philosophy of music education is consistent with that of the school, and also that it is not expressed in a way that either patronizes or mystifies any of the teaching staff. A scheme that does not explain why teachers or teaching assistants are expected to lead particular musical activities patronizes them, and can leave them feeling hopeless. If they do not know what pupils are intended to learn from a particular activity, and how they can recognize, and build upon, this learning, it is questionable whether the activity justifies any time that is spent on it.

Balancing the curriculum

Performing, composing, and listening all need high profiles in the music curriculum because they are the three fundamental activities of musicians. Moreover, many teachers assess pupils' progress using these headings. Hence we talk about balancing the curriculum. But this does not mean that equal time allocations need necessarily be given to composing, performing, and listening. This may be an effective way of organizing balance. Equally, it may not. What is needed is an adequate amount of time to listen, compose, and perform properly. The planning team will need to make their own decision about what this means. To give an example from elsewhere in the curriculum, is it more important that a child should be able to cross a road safely, or that she should be able to catch a ball? Most people would agree that being able to cross a road safely is at least as important as being able to catch a ball. So why do pupils spend more of their time in school catching balls, rather than practising road safety? Mainly because it is generally agreed that pupils can be taught road safety in less time.

Meaningful progression

As well as their freedom over content, teachers have more freedom concerning progression in music than in some other subjects. Teachers have the task of deciding how to move pupils up to at least Level 4 of the National Curriculum by the end of their time at primary school. There are many ways in which pupils could be encouraged to progress as musicians; it is likely that different schools will reach differing conclusions. However, the progression that teachers need to build into their teaching, and into pupils' response, must be musical progression. Pupils must become progressively better composers, performers, and listeners. Progression in composing, for instance, is achieved through making greater demands of pupils as composers—by helping them to become better at organizing sounds, and patterns of sound, to produce compositions. Pupils who have composed in response to a wide range of stimuli from their earliest days in school often make substantial progress as composers of their own accord. The matter of deciding how to move them still further forward often becomes much clearer when they are present, and composing (see p. 46).

When planning for progression, we often structure learning so that it moves from the simple to the complex. We teach pupils to count before they add. We teach them to add before they multiply. We teach recorder players to play at least one or two isolated notes before we move on to melodies.

Progression from simple to complex often makes a lot of sense. But not all learning is amenable to this sort of organization. Some learning takes place holistically. A word may be read at sight, rather than as a combination of letters. A painting may be appreciated, at least initially, as a whole, not as a combination of brush strokes. A piece of music may be responded to intuitively. We would not think of expecting pupils to understand all the components of a piece—the structures, techniques, and concepts it embodies—before we played them the piece itself.

Simple to complex progression is effective only when the constituent steps are meaningful. In music, this means that each step must be musical. Otherwise, breaking learning down into supposed simple units can result in pupils being asked to develop skills that are unmusical, and which may actually have to be unlearnt before the child can progress. Percy Scholes (Arnold 1984) summed up this problem in a comment on the use of associations between individual notes and colours to promote music reading: 'there seems to be little to be said for the practice, which, apparently, is merely an illustration of the way in which ingenious and kindly teachers often complicate comparatively simple subjects by inserting unnecessary steps.' Allowing young composers to use only the usual pentatonic scale (see p. 45) is another example of well-intentioned, but inappropriate, structuring of learning. Once pupils find that they do not have enough notes to play the melodies they know from the world outside, they may stop playing by ear. Having found that nothing sounds dreadful in this pentatonic scale, they may stop listening to what they compose. Consequently, when pupils are finally allowed to use any notes, they have to relearn listening and playing by ear. In other words, initial pentatonic composing does not simplify composing in any musical manner. In the longer term, it makes composing more complicated than necessary.

Of course composing is learnt progressively, and the teacher can provide structure, in a musical sort of way, to promote progression. But this can start from some observation of where the pupils are as composers, followed by thought about how they might move forward. If the pupils seem to be confused by having too many notes, try cutting them down occasionally—but not necessarily to a pentatonic scale. Would we try to develop pupils' writing by restricting the letters or words they had available for months on end? Imagine a school where the youngest pupils use only blue paint, with red being introduced at the age of 8, yellow a year later, and mixing at the age of 10!

A related problem arises when young children are given only a narrow range of instruments on which to compose and perform, and then introduced over several years to instruments which they could well have been playing since they were toddlers. In particular, young children are occasionally denied access to instruments that can produce loud, as well as soft, sounds (e.g. cymbals), instruments that produce low sounds (e.g. bass metallophones), or chromatic instruments—that is, instruments which include the piano black as well as white notes. I have never heard a convincing musical argument for this practice. Young pupils have no difficulty working with a wide range of dynamics, pitch, and notes. Five-year-olds are not too young to start learning to select a dynamic range appropriate to the task in hand, to practise discriminating between low notes, or to pick out or compose melodies that use black and white notes. If pupils are denied this experience in school, this simply increases the advantage of those who have it at home. They are less likely to become confused when the chromatic xylophone first appears when they are 7, or to go berserk when they get their first chance to hit a cymbal at the age of 8, or to say that they cannot hear the difference between low metallophone notes first presented when they are 9. They do not suffer the dips in their progress which are almost inevitable for less fortunate pupils.

A further example of inappropriate structuring is the provision of a listening diet that excludes contemporary classical music. Here, pupils are deprived, on grounds of supposed simplicity, of some music which young pupils, as open-minded listeners, do not seem to find particularly difficult. But by the time pupils are introduced to contemporary music, they have developed a taste which excludes it: they have to relearn open-minded listening. Listening to some music has been made more difficult, in the interests of simplicity.

In all of these examples, an attempt at simplification causes a dip (or U shape) in progress at some later stage. U-shaped behavioural growth has been observed in pupils' development in many fields. It is used to account for pupils', at least temporary, loss of apparent artistic flair as they become pre-occupied with representational drawing (Gardner and Winner 1982). It may be that dips are sometimes an inevitable part of progression. Progress may sometimes have to halt whilst a child grapples with a new concept that he or she could not have accommodated earlier. But going through dips is unpleasant, time-consuming, and potentially demotivating. There is no point in instituting unnecessary dips. Sequential learning has its place in music. But sequence should be derived from some sort of natural, musical, progression. It should not involve pupils in learning misinformation, disinformation, or unmusical skills which have only to be unlearnt later. Nor should it constrain the musical growth of pupils at any stage in their school career.

Meaningful assessment

When teachers write reports on pupils' progress in music, it makes sense for these to be as helpful as possible for parents and carers.

One low-energy approach to reporting is to repeat lots of words from the National Curriculum, but fail to frame them in such a way that informs parents and carers how their pupils are doing, and what they could do to help their child in future.

Here are some examples based on the version of the National Curriculum that applied from 1995 to 2000. The parents of Ahmed, a 7-year-old at school in England, might receive the following report:

Ahmed can perform simple rhythmic and melodic patterns by ear and from symbols. He can sing in a group and play simple instruments demonstrating some control of the sounds made. He can investigate, choose, and combine sounds to produce simple compositions, and can record his own compositions and communicate them to others. He can listen attentively and respond to short pieces of music from different times and cultures and in different styles, showing an awareness of differences and similarities. He can talk in simple but appropriate terms about sounds and music he has made, listened to, performed or composed.

The second sentence of the report of Belinda, one of the rare 7-year-olds who has still to find her singing voice, might read:

She has still to learn to sing in a group, but can play simple instruments demonstrating some control of the sounds made.

Neither Ahmed nor his parents would learn much from his report. Ahmed is clearly doing all right in music. But what, his parents might wonder, has he been doing? And what are his strengths? Belinda and her parents learn slightly more. But the extra information they receive is of a negative kind.

Clearly, the addition of some examples of what Ahmed and Belinda had been doing would enliven these accounts, and help to inform the readers about the context in which the pupils demonstrated the achievements reported. Teachers may find it helpful to reorder the statement to provide a more coherent account. They may wish to show, through the examples they choose, that they notice and build on pupils' achievement outside, as well as inside, school. Ahmed's report might become:

Ahmed sings with a good sense of pitch and a pleasant tone. He enjoys singing with a group of friends, and knows over 30 songs from memory. He shows imagination when exploring the sounds which can be made with instruments, and has devised some symbols to represent some unusual sounds he has found. He handles instruments with care, and is learning to use beaters better when playing xylophones and metallophones. He has recorded three of his compositions onto the enclosed cassette. He will be able to tell you about them, and explain how his score for one of them works. He showed patience when working on the melody for tenor xylophone, refining his ideas, and recording his work several times to get the effect he wanted. In his song, he has drawn on some chants learnt at football matches. He sometimes chooses to listen again to short pieces which we have listened to as a class, and often recognizes pieces that he heard some weeks previously.

This report is a little longer than the previous version, but much more use to Ahmed and his parents. It is also more use to his teacher. Set alongside the cassette to which it refers, and probably also some other recordings of Ahmed's work, it provides a basis for evaluating Ahmed's progress.

The success of this style of assessment depends on the regular recording of pupils' work. But then recording also promotes progression, for a composition or performance which is not recorded is often soon forgotten. And, as the National Curriculum in music provides for pupils to record their own work, teachers should find that much of the responsibility for recording can be devolved to pupils.

Implementing a curriculum plan

Curriculum plans always leave room for some degree of flexible implementation. Midway through realization of a plan, an unpredicted response from a child can lead to a change in direction of teaching. This may be a minor detour, or a complete change of route. It may lead to minute adjustment of aims, or a complete rethink of purpose. Planning, preparation, and experience all help a teacher to capitalize on pupils' response in a way that is likely to be productive. But they never result in a teacher being able to determine exactly how a lesson, let alone a longer period, will run.

I tend to think of the aims of curriculum planning in music as a series of layers, rather like those of an onion. The outer layer is the most abstruse, and yet the most important. It is to do with pupils' overall development as musicians: as listeners, performers, and composers. Moving inwards, subsequent layers define musical development in terms that become progressively more immediate. A layer close to the outer layer might be to do with aims for the year. Moving further in, we have the aims of the term, and then finally those for the lesson. Each lesson is planned within the terms of all these other layers. When pupils' response to a lesson surprises us, we break out of the immediate layer into a higher-order one so as to maintain overall musical development. A plan for a series of compositions about the seasons may be abandoned when the first composition, *Winter*, shows an exciting use of timbre which we want to develop without the constraint of thinking about summer. A plan to work on a Hallowe'en composition over several weeks may be discarded when the stimulus fails to set the pupils alight, or they quickly produce a work which is complete, though perhaps not on the grand scale we had anticipated. Ultimately, what matters is pupils' musical development, and we can sacrifice elements of our more closely defined musical concerns in order to achieve that. I repeat, for emphasis, a brief quotation from John Paynter that sums this up:

I have to say, in the end, I think that all that matters in music education is that what we do is musical. I don't care what it is. I would applaud whatever was happening in a classroom provided it was actually involving children in musical experience. (Salaman 1988: 31)

Beyond the layer I called musical development is a still more fundamental one—perhaps the onion skin—of development in general. As primary teachers we are concerned with all aspects of pupils' development in school. Music is a special and crucial part of this, but still only a part. In Chapter 8 we set music in the context of the primary curriculum.

Chapter 8

Music within the curriculum

The primary curriculum in England is changing rapidly at present. Had I started to write this new edition of *Music in the Primary School* five years ago, this chapter might have looked very different. At the time 'topics', through which most—or all—subjects were taught seemed to be a notion of the past. Schools in England were encouraged to teach a curriculum that was organized in separate lessons for each National Curriculum subject. Moreover, music was typically heard only in the afternoons, as the mornings were reserved for the crucial National Curriculum 'core' subjects of English and mathematics, or 'literacy' and 'numeracy' as they became known. This was because the morning was the time of day when pupils were thought to be more alert. But over the last year or so there has been more official recognition that while pupils may be learning to read and count better, they were enjoying doing it less. This is one of the reasons why, as I write, there is talk of a resurgence of 'topics' in primary schools. Quite what form that resurgence will take is unclear at this time. But we may soon start to see more of the curriculum organization that we remember from our own days in primary school, or our earlier days in teaching.

In this chapter, we set music in its wider context—the primary curriculum—and consider three of the issues this raises. First, we look at music within whole curriculum initiatives: topic work, or thematic work, as they are sometimes called. In the past, music appeared within topics less frequently than some other subjects (National Curriculum Council 1989). I take the view that what is good for other subjects is probably good for music too, and give some examples which show the range of possible approaches to music within topic work. Second, I illustrate the potential for music every-where by looking at some of the music that lies within science. Finally, I touch on the use of music as a means to another end. How can music be used as a learning medium? This is an issue that has become more topical in recent years. I take a particular example: music in language development, and then write more generally.

During this chapter, we return on several occasions to one dominant theme: the musical purpose of musical activity. However we are thinking of music at any particular time—as a subject, an element of science, or a learning medium—the music can be done musically. Even at times when our first priority for a child is not musical development, but learning to read, or scientific understanding, the music can be organized so as to take pupils forward as musicians: as composers, performers, or listeners. Cross-curriculum work is about enrichment, not compromise.

Music in topic work

Music, as we shall see, could be involved in topic work in many different ways. But, often, it is not there at all. Why is this? If we believe that cross-curriculum work is a viable approach to the primary curriculum, why should music be left out? Usually, music's exclusion from topics is just a matter of habit. Here, my intention is to show the range of possible approaches. Whether music *should* feature in any particular topic is a decision that a teacher will make after due consideration of topic coherence, and whether the pupils' current musical needs are best responded to within or beyond the topic. My purpose is to show that music *could* be involved in any topic. Music can be organized as flexibly as any other subject.

Schools and teachers may differ in their approach to topic work. Sometimes the topic *is* the curriculum; in other cases the topic serves as a temporary focus, with some work in most subject areas taking place outside it. Whatever the approach, music can take the same role as other subject areas.

Music's role in topics can sometimes be a little tokenistic. Whereas the contribution of other subjects to the topic has been carefully thought out with a view to pupils' development in the subject and throughout the topic, music may consist simply of listening material or songs chosen because of some relationship between the title and the topic. Songs and listening material can form part of a useful approach, but only if there is a musical reason for them being there. We need to be able to justify planned musical activity in terms of pupils' anticipated development as composers, performers, or listeners. The musical activities available are much wider than just songs and listening material with the right title. Any activity that we might think of including in a music lesson is, in principle, open to us. What is needed is musical *and* topic-related validity.

Below, I give some examples of activities that took place as part of music's contribution to various topics. Described without the context of their topics, they may sometimes sound contrived; in practice they were not. This list is not intended to provide an agenda for music in any topic you might think of. It is only a selection of the possibilities. In any topic, some activities are more appropriate than others. The list is intended simply to act as a stimulus for your own ideas.

A game
EXAMPLE   TOPIC: *Dinosaurs*

The pupils played a board game based on a published game called Prehistoric Ramble. Whilst the die was thrown, the class sang a special dinosaur song. Some squares on which the counter might land had instructions for a composition to describe a particular species of dinosaur. The teacher adapted the game by reducing the number of dinosaurs, rewriting some of the composing instructions to reflect the language level of her class of 7-year-olds, and replacing the published dinosaur song with one that the class already knew.

Performing
EXAMPLE   TOPIC: *Growth*

The class sang *The Runaway Seed* (see p. 64), a song with words written by their teacher.

EXAMPLE   TOPIC: *Time*

The class sang *Ticking Clocks*, a published round (Gadsby and Harrop 2002) which includes fast and slow ostinati.

Listening
EXAMPLE   TOPIC: *The Weather*

The class listened to the storm sections from each of the following pieces:
Richard Strauss: *Alpine Symphony*
Britten: *Four Sea Interludes*
Rossini: Overture to *William Tell*
Grieg: *Peer Gynt*

These extracts were chosen because the composer's stimulus lies within the topic and the teacher is convinced that the extracts are storm-like. Thus she presented them positively and, had the pupils not heard the relationship with storms, would have been able to explain why she found them convincing. She chose not to play the storm sections from Vivaldi's 'Summer' from *The Four Seasons*, or from Beethoven's 'Pastoral' Symphony because she finds them less convincing as storms.

EXAMPLE   TOPIC: *Growth*

The teacher played a recording of Pachelbel's *Canon*. Pachelbel is not known to have written this piece in response to a stimulus of growth. However, it audibly grows. Because the piece is a canon, it starts as a simple melodic line, with the other parts entering progressively. Thus, a multi-layered structure grows. The feeling of growth is strengthened by the tendency of later sections to include faster melodic patterns. The teacher feels a particular aesthetic response to this piece. She describes this by saying that, to her, the music has become more than the sum of its parts. She uses the analogy of a growing onion: the layers developing as the onion grows correspond to the new melodic entries. But the onion is an entity, not just a series of layers.

The pupils became very fond of this piece too, and often asked to hear it. After they had heard it several times, the teacher talked a little about the onion analogy. Explaining this too early might have rushed the pupils into hearing the piece only in the way that she does.

Composing

Composing is a highly adaptable activity. Whenever it is appropriate for pupils to be engaged in creative writing, they probably could be composing.

EXAMPLE TOPIC: *Fire*

After sitting by a real fire on a cold, dark day, and following a discussion, the pupils were asked to compose a piece entitled *The Real Fire*. The groups chose to emphasize some different aspects: the flickering light, the ever-changing images in the flames, the crackling sounds, the way in which you can become boiling hot on one side yet stay cold on the other, and the comfort of sitting by a fire when the weather outside is awful.

As the *flickering* group performed their piece to the rest of the class, another child spontaneously made a few *flickering* movements. Thus the music developed naturally into music/dance. First, the composers played their piece whilst another group moved. The dancers soon found that the piece moved between sections too fast for coherent movement to be possible. Next, the composers improvised around patterns from their piece whilst the dancers *flickered*. This improvisation took off. Individual musicians responded to the movement and to each other. The dancers responded to each other as well as to the music. Unfortunately this was not captured on video, and many ideas were forgotten. But the musicians and dancers together drew from what they remembered to draft a coherent piece of music/dance which gradually took on a more stable form.

The teacher found that the music about the comfort of sitting by a fire on a cheerless day made her think of another piece which was similarly inspired: the second movement of 'Winter' from Vivaldi's *The Four Seasons*. In this piece, a smooth and song-like melody on the solo violin is accompanied quietly by throbbing cellos, with the first and second violins playing a fast, but even, pizzicato (plucked) figure. The viola part, which is very slow-moving and sustained, seems to glue the whole piece together. The line of poetry that Vivaldi wrote above this music suggests the quiet contentment of someone sitting by the fire whilst it rains outside. The teacher thinks of the solo violin line as representing a dreaming, solitary, listener. The pizzicato figure suggests the flickering of the flames (or is it the rain on the roof?) whilst the violas, cellos, and bass provide warmth. She told the class about the line of poetry, and then played the piece. The composers commented thoughtfully about the similarities and differences of their piece and Vivaldi's. They thought that Vivaldi's use of sustaining instruments had enabled him to create a better feeling of warmth and contentment than they had. However, perhaps partly because they were so well inside their own piece, they thought that their less even use of gliding movements on a glockenspiel gave a more realistic impression of the firelight.

EXAMPLE TOPIC: *Growth*

The class had been reading and writing poems which 'grew'. Sarah, aged 8, used the plan of *This is the House that Jack Built* for her poem, *This is the Honey that Sarah Collected*. She wrote six verses. The first verse consisted of just one line. Subsequent verses consisted of the preceding verse with a new line added at the beginning. The class used Sarah's poem as the stimulus for a class composition. The longest verse had six lines, about the planting of seeds, the effect of the sun and rain, the opening of the flower, the collection of pollen by the bee, the departure of the bee to the hive, and Sarah's collection of honey from the hive. So the class divided into six groups, one to work on each line. Once the music had been devised, the teacher and class talked about the most effective way of organizing the whole composition. They experimented with a variety of solutions:

1. Sarah read the poem at a normal pace, and each line was accompanied by its music.

   The pupils rejected this idea because their music was often only half complete when Sarah moved to a new line. The music was losing its sense.

2. Sarah read each line at a normal pace, but paused between lines until the music had finished.

   The pupils did not like the way in which the verses were being chopped up. The poem was losing its sense.

3. The music and poem were separated. Sarah read the first verse, and then the first verse was played. Sarah read the second verse, and then the second verse was played, one line after the other, and so on.

   The pupils thought that this was an improvement, but wanted to organize the music so that it sounded less segmented.

4. They kept the same basic structure: verse 1 (poem), verse 1 (music), verse 2 (poem), etc. But the music was restructured. Instead of each line stopping when the next one came in, it was repeated as necessary until the last line of the verse was complete. Thus the last musical line of the sixth verse consisted of six layers of music.

   Now the pupils wanted to blur the edges between the spoken and played sections, and to decrease the length of the music, particularly for the later verses.

5. They kept the same basic structure: verse 1 (poem), verse 1 (music), etc. But the music for verse 1 played, very quietly, throughout the composition. Musical lines did not wait for the previous one to be completed, but entered after a decent interval. Balance, and points of entry, were controlled by a conductor.

   This was the final version.

Working between subjects

EXAMPLE TOPIC: *Our town*

The class visited their parish church. The atmosphere of the ancient stone-built structure, with its vaulted roof, characteristic smell, and bright stained-glass windows contrasting sharply with the semi-darkness, made an impact on many of the pupils. Whilst they sat quietly in the pews, the organist had started to practise.

Once back at school, some pupils responded to the visit by writing and drawing. Another group decided to compose instead. Impressed by the low sounds of the organ, and the reverberation time of the church, the pupils chose instruments that produce low sustaining sounds: a bass xylophone, an electronic keyboard, and a cello. Their piece was slow, solemn, and sustained.

EXAMPLE TOPIC: *Pattern*

Some pupils had been investigating the Four-Colour Problem. After many hours of experiment, they gradually became convinced that, whatever pattern you draw, you never need more than four colours to arrange so that no two areas with a common boundary are the same colour. They became interested in what they saw as the distinctiveness of the number four. They chose four xylophone notes—B(lue), C(herry), E(cru), and G(reen)—and started to assemble four-note melodies according to rules that they devised: adjacent notes must be different, and the melody must be interesting.

Music within science

There is potential for music in any subject. Here, I take science as an example.

There are many phenomena which interest both musicians and scientists. For example:

- Music exists as sound within time.
- We hear music through our ears.
- Music is dependent on materials, and the methods by which they are played.
- Our perception of music is determined by several factors, including our position relative to a sound source, and the acoustics of the environment.
- People with impaired hearing respond to music.
- Guitar frets get closer together towards the bridge because of the roughly logarithmic relationship between pitch and frequency.
- Our perception of high notes deteriorates with age, and after listening to loud music.
- Horn players who sit at the back of an orchestra find that they need to make a conscious effort to play ahead of the beat that they hear from the first violins.
- We can predict the fundamental note of a tuba by measuring its vibrating length, and then measure the error of our prediction using our ears.
- We can predict where a violin string should be stopped to produce a particular harmonic, and account for inaccuracy in terms of the inflexibility of strings.
- We can use computer software to synthesize an oboe tone, harmonic by harmonic.

All these topics can be taught in a mode which is musical as well as scientific. But I shall focus on a narrow area of commonality between science and music in the primary curriculum. In Table 1, I give the part of the Programmes of Study for science in the National Curriculum (DfEE and QCA 1999b) that relates to sound (Sc4 Physical processes), and make suggestions about how the scientific content might be developed or reinforced musically. Many of my suggestions are for listening, often in combination with looking. Most suggestions amount to little more than encouraging pupils to observe the effects of their investigations with their ears as well as their eyes. Listening could, of course, lead to performing and composing whenever the teacher wished. My suggestions tie in with the current National Curriculum for music in England.

Many of my suggestions for music are very similar to those in Part I; the music that overlaps with science is not special music. Very few of my musical suggestions are not scientific too. This is a powerful illustration of how working between subjects can save time. It cannot, on its own, provide a music education which is systematic or adequate. One could not hope to teach music by only teaching science. But musical interpretation of the science National Curriculum can mean that pupils reinforce their scientific learning, and arrive at music sessions better prepared. Activity in music really can stimulate, and be stimulated by, activity in science. And, of course, the same is true for other pairs of subjects.

Table 1 Suggestions for music using the Programmes of Study (Sc 4 Physical processes) for Science in the National Curriculum (DfEE and QCA, 1999b), Key Stages 1 and 2

Science programmes of study	Suggestions for music
KEY STAGE 1 Reception–Year 2	
Making and detecting sounds	1 Close listening to these sounds (e.g. 'Sit quietly for a minute . . . What did you hear?).
◆ That there are many kinds of sound and sources of sound	2 Describing sounds (e.g. 'How is Mark's sound different from Julie's sound? . . . Yes, it is faster . . . Claire said it was brighter, too. Claire, can you find me a sound which is brighter still?').
◆ That sounds travel away from sources, getting fainter as they do so.	3 Identifying sounds of which the sources are hidden (e.g. 'What is the noise we can hear from outside? . . . Is it a car or a motorbike?' or 'Peter is sitting round the corner with some instruments. When he starts to play one, I'd like you to pick the same instrument from this set here and copy him.')
	4 Experimenting on improvised and purchased instruments.
	5 Composing using resources defined according to the method of sound production (e.g. 'Here are some different types of elastic bands, and some boxes of different sizes. See how many different plucked sounds you can make . . . Tony played us a melody on his bands . . . What other melodies can you make?).
	6 Investigating the effect of playing instruments in unconventional ways (e.g. blowing into the holes of a guiro).
	7 Making recordings of sounds made in various ways for other pupils to identify.

Continued

Table 1 Continued

Science programmes of study	Suggestions for music

KEY STAGE 2 Year 3–Year 6

Pupils should be taught:

◆ That sounds are made when objects [for example, strings on musical instruments] vibrate but that vibrations are not always directly visible

◆ How to change the pitch and loudness of sounds produced by some vibrating objects [for example a drum skin, a plucked string]

◆ That vibrations from sound sources require a medium [for example, metal, wood, glass, air] through which to travel to the ear.

1 Further experimenting with improvised and purchased instruments.

2 Further investigation of how instruments work.

3 Experimenting and performing on *stringed instruments:*

◆ Noticing which end of a stopped string vibrates, visually and by touch.

◆ Hearing the effect of damping a vibrating string.

◆ Investigating the relationship between pitch and vibrating length.

◆ Noting that lower strings are thicker.

◆ Investigating the effect of tension on the pitch of a plucked elastic band.

◆ Feeling the vibration in the sound box of a guitar.

◆ Considering the differing duration of plucked and bowed strings.

And so on.

4 Experimenting and performing on *wind instruments*:

◆ Noting that lower instruments are typically larger.

◆ Tuning a set of milk bottles to give a melody when blown across by adjusting the amount of water they contain.

◆ Listening to the effect of embouchure on the precise pitch of a milk-bottle note.

◆ Blowing and overblowing recorders.

And so on.

5 Experimenting and performing on *percussion instruments:*

◆ Choosing beaters to give a particular effect.

◆ Listening to the unevenness caused when using an unmatched pair of beaters.

◆ Noticing that drums and so on do have a pitch.

◆ Observing the inside of a piano: the effects of the pedals, hammers and dampers, the gradation of string length and thickness, duplication and triplication of strings.

And so on.

6 Investigation of selective listening (e.g. 'Rajiv, hit the
  cymbal and tell us when it has become silent . . .
  Those of us who were further away from the cymbal
  thought that it had finished when it was still going
  . . . What did you hear while we were waiting for
  Rajiv? . . . Richard said he could hear the traffic . . .
  Do you usually notice the traffic, Richard? . . . Why
  do you think you noticed it then? . . . Tanya says
  that the traffic is annoying her now').

Music as a learning medium

There are many situations in which music may be used as a learning medium,
not just as an end in itself. Counting songs can be used to reinforce number
concepts. In music therapy, music is used as a means of communication
between therapist and client. I shall take just one particular example: the promotion of language development through music. As language and music are
both concerned with sound, they have some common basis. I shall outline two
psychological studies which look at language development and music from
different angles. The first, by Audrey Wisbey, concerns the relationship
between childhood hearing loss and difficulties with language development.
The second by Peter Bryant and Lynette Bradley, considers the relationship
between the ability to rhyme and alliterate and reading development. Though
Bryant and Bradley write about sound awareness in a general, not just musical, sense, their work has implications for music education.

Audrey Wisbey's theories received extensive media coverage in the early
1980s. Whilst a teacher, Wisbey became concerned by the number of apparently intelligent pupils who fail to become literate. In *Music as the Source of
Learning* (Wisbey 1980), she attributes the literacy difficulties of many pupils
to hearing problems including common ailments such as catarrh, sinusitis,
and infected tonsils in early childhood. Even when pupils' residual hearing is
assessed as 'within the limits or normality', there can be serious hearing loss of
high-frequency sounds. This can result, Wisbey believes, in insufficient or
inaccurate learning of speech sounds. By the time that the cause of the hearing
problem is diagnosed and attended to, the child will have lost some
high-frequency hearing through ageing; thus it can be too late for pre-literacy
auditory learning to take place. The relationship between hearing and language learning is probably two-way; Leontiev (1969) attributed the superior
pitch discrimination ability of some Vietnamese people to the tonal nature
of their language. Unlike people whose language is less tonal, their pitch

discrimination did not deteriorate when tones were presented using the usually difficult 'u' and 'e' sounds instead of pure tones.

Wisbey emphasizes the importance of early music education. It facilitates the identification of hearing problems, and reinforces learning of the sounds that form the components of speech. Her approach to music education is controlled, systematic, and progressive. Pupils work with the raw ingredients of music—pitch, duration, intensity, timbre, rhythm, and so on—and learn simple sounds before moving on to more complex ones. I would quibble with some details of her method. In *Learn to Sing to Learn to Read* (Wisbey 1981), for instance, the simple to complex progression is applied even to the number of notes that pupils use. For some weeks, the pupils use only middle C. This would seem to me to be potentially boring, and difficult to justify as neither music nor language requires the ability to recall or identify precise pitches, sometimes known as absolute pitch or perfect pitch. But many of the activities, which include careful listening often combined with spatial awareness, are very valuable. Many are similar to those suggested in the section on music within science. The important difference is that Wisbey believes these activities should commence in early childhood—long before they would be encountered in science lessons.

In *Children's Reading Problems*, Peter Bryant and Lynette Bradley (1985) report their findings that 'backward' readers are often very poor at detecting rhyme and alliteration. In particular, pupils who are poor rhymers at the age of 4 or 5 tend to be poorer readers and spellers at the age of 8 or 9. This result is independent of the tested intelligence of the pupils concerned. This led Bryant and Bradley to pose two questions. Can pupils be taught to rhyme and alliterate? If so, does this, on its own, improve their reading? The answer to both questions was 'yes'. Sixty-five pupils aged 6 were divided into four groups. During 40 sessions over two years, Group 1 was taught about rhyme and alliteration. Within the same time allocation, Group 2 was taught also to relate rhyme and alliteration to their reading. Group 3 was a taught control group; the members attended 40 special sessions over two years, but were taught material other than rhyme and alliteration. Group 4 was a control group which had no special experimental tuition. At the end of the two-year period, the pupils in Group 2 were found, allowing for other factors, to have a reading age that was six months greater than Group 1, ten months greater than Group 3, and fourteen months greater than Group 4. Thus learning to rhyme and alliterate improved reading, but the greater improvement occurred when the rhyming and alliteration were applied specifically to reading.

Rhyming and alliteration can be developed in many ways. Bryant and Bradley used pictures of named objects. Drawing attention to rhyme in the

lyrics of songs, including nursery rhymes, could help with language development. Indeed, the National Curriculum for English in England includes the
use of songs (DfEE and QCA 1999c).

The work of Bryant and Bradley, and that of Wisbey, indicates the use of
music as a learning medium in language development. This is constructive for
music as well as language: when the singing of rhymes, and learning about the
parameters of music, is handled musically, then musical development is taking
place at the same time as language development. But consideration of these
studies reminds us—if we ever needed to be reminded—that we cannot
organize the curriculum for any subject, be it music, language, or science, simply by relying on experience in other subject areas. According to Wisbey, it
seems that the music included in the National Curriculum for science will take
place too late for it to be of much value in promoting pupils' verbal literacy.
Bryant and Bradley's findings that the best gains in reading ability were
obtained when rhyming and alliteration were applied to reading indicate that
singing nursery rhymes, alone, will not maximize the potential of rhyme to
increase pupils' reading ability. Cross-curriculum work offers marvellous
opportunities for counting time at least twice. But subject-specific development cannot take place through haphazard encounter in other subject
areas. Musical development through music-language, music-science, or
music-anything requires specific musical relevance.

In recent years, there have been some less measured claims for the benefits
of music in general in education. In 1998, Katie Overy (1998) tried to redress
the balance by inviting researchers to address the question 'Can music really
"improve" the mind?' within the pages of *Psychology of Music*. Six responses
were published, of which mine ran:

Katie Overy asks, 'can music really "improve" the mind?' Note that she asks '*can* it?', not
'*does* it?'

These are two very different questions. As I understand it, Katie Overy is asking
whether there are circumstances or conditions, perhaps a particular sort of music or a
style of music teaching, under which music may improve the mind. She is not asking
whether any sort of experience that could sit under the general heading of 'music'
always improves the mind.

The 'does' question has recently attracted considerable interest in educational circles
in England. Rightly or wrongly, some musicians and music educators have thought
that the place of music in our National Curriculum was under threat, and have sought
to defend it by arguing that music offers psychological benefits that extend beyond the
realms of the subject. Some of this defence has been responsible, careful and thoughtful. However, there have been examples of carefully crafted research findings being
taken out of their context and over-generalised to the point that music, any music, has
been portrayed as a panacea. Researchers have been commissioned to investigate
whether or not music is a panacea. In fact the 'does' assertion is easy and not costly to

refute. One just needs to find a single counter-example of music failing to improve the mind, an example of 'does not' and it has bitten the dust. I suspect that we can all think of an example of 'does not' from our own experience. Depending on our prejudices, we may need to look no further than the nearest rave, radio station, supermarket or crush bar for our counter-example. The 'can' question is much more interesting.

Katie Overy mentions a study in Switzerland (Spychiger *et al.*, 1993). This is an appealing study if only because of the audacity, given the usual hierarchy of subjects, of the finding that the pupils who did more music in school, at the expense of language and mathematics, became better at language and reading and no worse at mathematics. Educationally, I do not think that it matters much whether motivation played as great a part as music in securing these results, because the motivation was bound up with the music. Spychiger showed that, in the particular circumstances of her investigation, the answer to the 'can' question is 'yes'. However, common sense tells us that this specific 'can' finding cannot be extended into a general 'does' finding. Were we to require all the schools in England to give pupils more music at the expense of mathematics and English we would soon find rather more than one counter-example of a school where standards in mathematics and English plummeted, if only because the teachers would not have been persuaded that this experiment was likely to work. Spychiger's study is interesting, not because it is generalisable, but because it questions the educationally unquestionable. It provides plenty of food for thought. For example, do mathematics teachers sometimes waste some of the relatively large amounts of time that they have at their disposal? And there may be aspects of Spychiger's study that are generalisable, if only we could isolate them. For example, what was it that led to improvements in language and reading skills, despite less time being available?

To return to Katie Overy's question, I have little doubt that music can, under particular circumstances, improve the mind. One need do no more than sit in the classroom of a really good music teacher who believes that music can improve the mind, and observe the pupils growing intellectually in front of your eyes to be convinced of this. What I am sometimes less certain about is what, exactly, this teacher is doing that leads to this improvement, and whether other teachers could be trained to do it too. If we are to exploit the potential of music to improve the mind, we need researchers, perhaps including inspectors, to help isolate the conditions under which this happens. Perhaps it helps if teachers have a particular sort of commitment. Perhaps it helps if the teaching is particularly sequential. Perhaps it helps if pupils are taught to perform from memory, or to sing at sight, or to try to refine their compositions through thought experiments, instead of always reaching for a keyboard. Doubtless there are a host of other possible factors. Perhaps we need just one of them to be in place. Perhaps we need them all. Once we know more we will need to establish whether these factors can be packaged in a music education that is excellent musically. If they cannot, then the investigation may have added to the sum of human knowledge, but will not be of educational value. Whatever the potential of music to improve the mind, the main purpose of teaching music in schools is excellence in music. (Mills 1998)

This debate continues today. A couple of years ago there was a fad for playing music as background for almost any form of learning in a primary school. It must have been obvious that while some pupils and teachers might like this, others might find it distracting. There was also a fad for labelling pupils as 'different sorts of learners' in a very simplistic way. I wrote the following for *Link* magazine. It starts with me in a primary school, working as a school inspector.

In defence of auditory learning

I enter the classroom. Pachelbel's *Canon* plays quietly in the corner. The pupils are working silently on number problems. I smile 'good morning' to the teacher, sit down by the files of lesson plans, individual education plans and assessment records that she has laid out for me, and begin to fill out my form:

> Year 6. Mathematics. 13 boys, 16 girls. Attainment target 2, levels 3–5. Pupils seated boy–girl in attainment groups with differentiated worksheets . . .

I can barely think. The Pachelbel is approaching the height of its beautiful, long, crescendo. I know this piece inside out. It draws me in. . . Get a grip on yourself, Mills. The teacher is playing this stuff because she believes it will help the pupils. They are coping. So can you.

But are they coping? It is the Minuet from *Berenice* now. A boy seated away from the CD player starts to caterwaul quietly with the melody. A girl nudges him to be quiet, with a worried look at me. I smile reassuringly. The boy looks to be in pain. He is struggling to complete his level 5 mathematics—at a fast pace, neatly and accurately—while this drug that is music courses through his mind. He is battling to concentrate, to do his work, to please his teacher, the girl, me. . .

A few minutes later, midway through a phrase of a Mozart horn concerto, the teacher turns off the music, and explains something mathematical to the whole class. She turns on the music again. It is the first movement of Vivaldi's 'Winter'.

What is going on here? Why is this keen, experienced and very able teacher making it so difficult for at least some of her class to do their mathematics? Why is she polluting their learning environment with music? What is her evidence that this use of music is helping anyone with their mathematics? Let alone helping them to develop as musicians?

In another ethnically diverse school, in another city, some secondary teachers have just returned from a course on learning styles. A handout explains how to use music to promote learning in any subject. Teachers should play baroque music to students engaged in repetitive tasks in order to discourage their creativity, romantic music including the Brahms *Brandenburg Concertos* [*sic*] when seeking to encourage creativity, and music with 'explosions' before potentially dangerous experiments in science. 'Auditory learners' should be seated away from the music, or issued with ear plugs.

The world is going mad. Some rigorous and, as I understand it, distinct pieces of research into the effect of playing Mozart to some particular learners, and individual learning styles, have been hijacked by well-meaning people who did not understand them fully, and turned into dogma that teachers are, seemingly, expected to apply blindly. The advantages of sending children to school each day, rather than plugging them into computers at home, include that schools have teachers who think.

And why is it (nearly) always western classical music that gets turned into dogma? Is this because children who are played djembe drumming, hip hop or samba smile, or move their shoulders rhythmically with the music, so that we cannot but notice our educational problem?

I am writing this at the Royal College of Music. Student practice streams into my room from all directions. Mendelssohn, Puccini, Chopin, John Coltrane, and something excitingly spiky and avant-garde from the percussion suite. . . This doesn't distract me from writing. Why not? Perhaps because it is practice, rather than perform-ance, so that I feel OK to drift in and out, even ignore it for minutes on end? But even as I suggest this, I can see holes. There are days when practice intrudes. This is partly a matter of mood, not what I am trying to do. And the sound of quiet practice at home, when I am trying to write, can drive me berserk.

Using music as a drug is educationally dangerous. We don't know what it does, but we do know that it does different things to different people, and different things to the same people at different times. And we can be fairly sure that different pieces of music do different things too. Education is not a career for witch doctors. As teachers, we need to understand what we are doing. (Mills 2004)

Music is not a panacea but an art. By teaching music in school, and teaching it in a way that is as positive, enabling, creative and artistic as possible, we help pupils to make the most of music, for themselves, as they move through life.

Chapter 9

Music within the primary school

Taking up an instrument seriously is like a life sentence.
Ronnie Scott, *Observer Sayings of the Week*, 5 August 1984

Up to now, we have focused on music within the common curriculum of primary pupils. In a sense, we have shut the classroom door, and ignored the world outside. In fact, curriculum music is often not the only music taking place in primary school. Many schools also offer additional activities for some pupils. These activities may take place outside class time, and may involve additional teachers, perhaps instrument teachers, visiting artists, or secondary music teachers. How can we see both class music and additional musical activities as operating within a coherent policy for school music? I start by reviewing my guidelines for primary music.

School music

In Chapter 1, I wrote of music in primary school as:

- an active subject consisting of the interdependent activities of listening, performing, and composing
- for all pupils and all teachers
- valuable only if enjoyable.

Hitherto, we have developed these ideas through thinking about music in classrooms. But how do voluntary additional activities such as choirs drawn from several classes, or compulsory additional activities led by visiting artists, fit in? In general, the additional activities operate within the same guidelines. The activities are concerned with at least one of composing, performing, or listening. They are open to all pupils and teachers. Observation of the pupils shows that they are enjoying themselves. But is there a coherent relationship between the class music and the additional activities? In some schools, the class music and extra activities are well integrated and mutually supporting. The voluntary activities—choirs, orchestras, instrument lessons, projects, and so on—enrich classroom music by enabling pupils to extend themselves according to individual interest and need. Pupils who particularly enjoy singing are able to do more than is possible during class time by joining a choir. Those ready to read music before their peers can learn to play the recorder, or another instrument, from notation. Those ready to learn an orchestral instrument are given the opportunity to do so. But although these activities take place at different times from classroom music, they do not take place independently. Instrumentalists bring their instruments into the classroom and use them during composing and performing activities. Their performance provides the stimulus for listening activity, and often results in more pupils wanting to take up instruments. The choir members' enthusiasm for singing becomes a catalyst for increased singing development in the class as a whole.

These extra activities are sometimes referred to as extra-curricular. This can give the impression that they are separate from the class music curriculum, rather than an extension of it. So here I refer to them as extension music.

In some schools, the classroom music and the extra activities are less well integrated. Two separate systems operate. All pupils receive classroom music, and some also participate in other activities. In some cases admission to extra-curricular groups is by interest, and in others pupils are selected. This is extra-curricular music in the most narrow sense of the term—music that literally lies outside the school's music curriculum. The independent operation of curricular and extra-curricular music, combined with the relatively high public profile that extra-curricular groups often have, can lead pupils, teachers, and parents to believe that extra-curricular music is more important. In fact, Susan O'Neill and I (Mills and O'Neill 2002) discovered that primary schools with a reputation for being 'musical' may have lower, rather than higher, standards for music in the school as a whole. A school music policy that values extra-curricular music above curriculum music is harmful. First, it is divisive: not all pupils participate in the higher-status activity. Pupils become divided into two groups, one of which is often termed 'musical', so that the other one comes to regard itself as 'unmusical'. Thus pupils view themselves as hopeless in music long before they have started to think about their ability in other subjects. Second, it can lead to curriculum music becoming less coherent. Teachers worn out by a high-priority series of extra-curricular activities may cut corners when it comes to curriculum music. Class music may be organized haphazardly and without attention to individual needs or progression; indeed, it may consist almost entirely of massed sing-songs or radio, CD, and video programmes. Communal singing is fun as a treat, but it is not an efficient way of developing the singing of the pupils who most need help, or stretching the more able. CD and video programmes can be a valuable resource for teachers to work round, but are never a replacement for a music curriculum designed to take account of individual differences and needs. Would teachers devolve responsibility for their entire mathematics curriculum to the BBC, or to an author who has been neither a teacher nor a mathematician?

There is no purpose in thinking about curricular and extra-curricular music separately. There is no voluntary activity that cannot take place, or standard that cannot be reached, within a model of school music in which curriculum music, the focus of activity, is enriched by extension music. Thinking about school music as a coherent whole ensures that all pupils receive the planned music education to which they are entitled.

Extension music

Extension music, then, consists of music activities that are additional to those participated in by the whole class. The instrument lessons often provided by visiting specialists are a component to which we turn later. Here, I focus on the extension activities led by school teachers, and visiting artists. Of what might these consist? This depends on the interests and expertise of the contributing staff and the pupils. Choirs, recorder groups, and orchestras are common. Some schools are resourced for pop groups and steel bands. In others, pupils and teachers meet regularly at lunchtimes to explore the links between music and dance, or to work with music computer software. Or artists visit the school, and give workshops to whole classes. The possibilities are limitless. The important point is that the extension music extends what is already going on in classrooms; it is not an alternative system.

Two questions about the organization of activities arise:

◆ Should membership be open or selected?

◆ Should casual attendance be permitted?

The answers to these questions depend on the nature of the activity. An instrumental group rehearsing systematically and progressively over several weeks for a performance requires consistent membership, but an instrumental group that meets weekly for one-off sessions does not. Membership may have to be restricted if there are not enough resources, such as keyboards to go round. Some activities may be designed with a particular group of pupils in mind, for instance some unusually advanced recorder players. But many activities can take place with open membership and casual attendance. In many schools, this mode of operation is the norm, with other modes being regarded as exceptions which need to be justified.

In the past, it was common for the members of choirs, for instance, to be selected. The membership of the choir at the junior school I attended was determined by a sort of compulsory audition. All pupils—whether we were interested in joining the choir or not—sang individually to our teacher in front of the rest of the class. As we had never sung solos in school before, many of us felt fairly foolish. At least we were not left in suspense as to the outcome of the audition. As soon as a solo was over, the soloist was directed to stand in one of two lines: the passes and the fails. Choir members had badges presented to them in assembly. We were told that the word choir was written in silver, not gold, lettering, as a mark of the light, silvery, quality of our voices. Brassy voices were out. I still have my badge somewhere, along with the attendance badge which I gained through being blessed with such good health that I had not been ill for an entire year.

The school choir met weekly to rehearse songs which we sang in non-competitive festivals. During daily assembly, we sat smugly on benches at the front, facing the pupils with brassy voices who were seated cross-legged on the floor. We marched out of the hall ahead of them. I enjoyed my time in the choir. Doubtless, I learnt a lot from it. But what good came from leaving out other pupils? Would they develop silvery voices by being given less opportunity to sing? Did the odd brassy voice matter, if we were not competing for anything? And were they all left unscarred by the daily reminder of their musical inferiority?

I left primary school in 1965, a time when competition was more a part of primary-school life than it is now. Set in the context of 11-plus examinations, streaming from the age of 7, termly form placings, and the dreaded annual sports days in which incompetents like myself had no option but to make public fools of themselves (whilst 'letting down' the blue team . . .), there was nothing particularly evil about the way in which the choir was organized. But whereas the 11-plus has all but disappeared, and sports days have become quite jolly affairs, here and there the selected choir still survives. Back in 1989, I visited a primary classroom where the sole list of pupils' names on the wall announced who had been selected by audition for the choir. Jonathan, aged 8, was not on the list. I asked him about his favourite songs. 'I am no good at singing', he said. Examples of Jonathan remain in schools today.

My argument for regarding open membership as the norm is to do with decreasing the number of pupils who label themselves as unmusical, and reducing the sort of competition that is futile. My case for regarding the possibility of casual attendance as the norm is different; primary age pupils are often not in a position to understand the musical and educational reasons for committed attendance. It is agreed that the progress of musical ensembles is usually greater when the total membership is present for every rehearsal. Ensemble playing is not just a matter of getting your notes right. An ensemble is not just a group of individuals whose playing is synchronized by a human starting-pistol sometimes known as a conductor. Ideally, an ensemble sounds and feels like a single composite instrument. This has to be practised; hence the advantage of consistent membership. The problem is that it is difficult for anyone to understand this if they have not been in an ensemble that has at least started to achieve the composite instrument feeling. Many younger primary pupils have not. If we do not let them join in some activities on a casual basis, at least to begin with, they may not come at all. That way, they will never come to appreciate the musical reasons for sustained attendance. And, more importantly, they will never have the experience of participating in ensemble performance.

Instrument teaching

What part can the instrument specialists who visit some schools play in school music? In some LAs, the specialists have been absorbed into Music Support Services which perform a number of functions, often including supporting the music curriculum work of primary class teachers. Here, the work of the school and the visiting teacher is already well integrated. This section is concerned particularly with the more traditional arrangement in which instrument teachers visit schools with the explicit purpose of teaching groups, and possibly individuals, to play instruments. At the current time there is also an expansion of whole-class programmes where instrument teachers and class teachers work together, sharing their expertise, to provide all pupils with the opportunity to learn an instrument. The range of instruments taught in many regions is wide. The examples in this section refer to systems in which teaching is almost exclusively confined to orchestral and band instruments in individual or small group situations. However, some of the points I make have wider applicability.

Instrument teaching sometimes operates completely independently of class teaching. The instrument teacher visits the school, gives lessons out of earshot, and then disappears into the distance. The only evidence of his or her presence is the periodic purposeful movement round the school of groups of pupils carrying violin cases.

This can be a great waste of an expensive resource. Even if the lessons are being paid for mainly by parents, pupils are contributing their time, and schools are giving their facilities. Pupils' musical development can become divided into two compartments—school music and instrument lessons—which may have little in common, or may overlap without purpose. The school as a whole does not gain from the presence of the instrument teachers.

Instrument lessons can be regarded as a form of extension music; an optional activity for pupils interested in developing as performers. Usually, instrument teachers welcome opportunities to meet with members of a school's music staff to plan this. Travelling round a series of schools all day, with little contact with adults, and little sustained contact with anyone, is a lonely business which can feel aimless. Links between instrument lessons and school music can commence with including instrument teachers in the discussion of school music policy and, where their terms of employment permit this, inviting instrument teachers to spend part of their time in school working with classes, or with extension activities such as orchestras. This can often lead to effective and early integration of instrumentalists into class music and other extension activities.

Instrument lessons, even when available without charge, often need to be made exceptions to the norms of casual attendance and open membership. If pupils do not attend lessons regularly, they are unlikely to make sustained progress. It would be difficult for instrument teachers, who are usually only in each school for a few hours each week, to build sufficient flexibility into their teaching to be able to accommodate ever-changing groups. Many schools seek parental support for sustained attendance before tuition commences. But pupils cannot be expected to understand the musical reasons for this if they have not had some previous experience of learning to play an instrument. Thus the option of instrument lessons is best preceded by opportunities to participate in activities organized on a more casual basis. Even with the very best of preparation, it is inevitable that some pupils will still want to give up lessons within a few weeks of starting. It is very difficult to know whether you are going to like playing the marimba until you have tried it. And no matter how carefully you explain to pupils that it will be many years before they become accomplished on marimba, some will still be bitterly disappointed when they are unable to emulate the performance of Evelyn Glennie within three or four weeks. Whilst encouraging pupils to regard instrument lessons as a commitment, we need to accept that some pupils will still want to give up. And overstressing the seriousness of taking up instrument lessons is not always in pupils' best interests. An example serves as an illustration:

Ann took up the violin in response to a fortunate second offer of lessons in school at the age of 12. Her first chance had been three years earlier. Interested pupils had been told to think seriously about whether they could guarantee that they would not want to give up. If so, they should tell their teacher. Ann obeyed these instructions to the letter. She thought seriously, realised that she could not guarantee that she would never want to give up, and so did not tell her teacher anything. Most of the 9-year-olds who took up the violin gave up within a term or so. Ann is now a successful violin teacher.

Ideally, instrument lessons would be open to everyone who wanted them. Perhaps school teachers might encourage the parents of pupils who seemed particularly keen to come forward. In fact, the fees that would be charged to parents may be too great for them to afford, or the supply of instruments and lesson time may be insufficient to cope with demand. In this case, selection for instrument lessons becomes inevitable. On what basis should it be made? This depends on the purpose of the instrument lessons. Are they intended to enrich the education of gifted musicians, such as those who will eventually become professional performers? If so, we need some sort of predictive test of musical ability. Or are they part of the musical extension offered optionally to all pupils? If so, we want to find the pupils who will get the greatest benefit (whatever we mean by this) from their lessons. In fact, these two views of the purpose of instrument lessons are not as incompatible as they might at first seem. The pupils who will become the professional performers of tomorrow are amongst those who will benefit from instrument lessons. Thus a selection system that aims to identify pupils who will most profit from lessons—musically, educationally, and socially—will, if it is successful, result in so-called gifted pupils, amongst a lot of other pupils, starting lessons.

Before deciding how to devise a system, it is useful to reflect on how we will measure its effectiveness. In the past, this has sometimes been assessed in terms of the proportion of pupils who continue lessons for sustained periods. Or rather, to be more accurate, ineffectiveness has been assessed in terms of the proportion of pupils giving up. Mawbey (1973) writes of 'the problem of wastage from instrumental classes', and attributes it to selection procedures which are insufficiently rigorous in, for instance, 'screening out those who have no musical talent'. The idea that an effective selection system is one in which there is little, or preferably no, drop-out has been implicit in more recent investigations.

I do not accept that a child who gives up instrument lessons necessarily forms evidence of the failure of a selection procedure. In fact, I have difficulty with the idea that effectiveness is about how long pupils continue with lessons, or the ultimate level of their performance. How long do pupils have to carry on before we judge them successes? Is a child who persists with violin tuition until she leaves school and then never touches a violin again a success? Is another who only takes flute lessons for two terms but then buys himself an electric guitar and forms a pop band a failure? How good do pupils have to get before we judge them successes? Do they have to be accepted into music college, or is a more modest performance level, perhaps Grade 5 of the examinations conducted by the Associated Board of the Royal Schools of Music, enough? If the former, then the success rate must be embarrassingly small in every LA throughout the country. If the latter, then we still have a problem: to what extent can Grade 5, for instance, be judged a mark of musical achievement? Grade 5 performers will still find most of the standard classical repertoire played by even the humblest local amateur orchestra well beyond their reach. The effectiveness of selection cannot be measured solely in terms of performing attainment or staying power. Pupils who end up accomplished performers *are* successes; but then so are those who have benefited in any other way from their lessons. These include pupils who have grown in confidence, or social skills, as well as those who have learnt the most modest of music skills which could act as the foundation for others in the future. This leads to measures of selection effectiveness which are more woolly than continuation rates or attainment levels. It means that we need to think of effectiveness in terms of what individuals have learnt, in the widest sense, through their lessons. But this is something which we have to accept if we think that instrument teaching is about extension for everyone, not just enrichment for the jet set. Perhaps initiatives such as peer assessment will help us to involve pupils more in the improvement of their work.

I have suggested the following:

◆ Instrument teaching should be available to those pupils who will benefit from it. This includes those whose ultimate musical achievement will be modest, as well as those who will eventually become highly accomplished musicians.

◆ Likely perseverance in instrument lessons is a quality to be valued. But it is not the be-all and end-all of successful selection.

◆ Pupils who give up tuition have not necessarily wasted their places.

That said, it makes sense to organize instrument teaching so that pupils are encouraged to continue with tuition, and make as much progress as possible. One of the ways of doing this is to give some consideration to whether individuals might be particularly suited to one instrument rather than another. The allocation of pupils to instruments is sometimes a little haphazard.

So how might allocation be organized? We want a system that selects persevering potential high-flyers, but does not screen out other keen pupils. We want pupils to end up playing the instruments on which they will make the most progress. There is no perfect way of organizing selection for anything. We just have to try to minimize the number of mistakes we make. And there is no ideal system of selecting pupils for instrument lessons which can be applied in all situations; those responsible have to decide how best to operate in their particular circumstances. But there are some steps which teachers can take to increase the validity of the criteria that they use when selecting, and, most importantly, pupils use when choosing.

1. Allow pupils to become familiar with several instruments before choosing one

Surprising though it may seem, some pupils arrive at their first instrument lesson without knowing what their chosen instrument either looks or sounds like. This cannot increase their chance of success. Suppose they do not like the sound? Suppose there is another instrument which makes a sound that they would prefer to make? Suppose there is no room for the cello on the minibus on which they travel to school each day?

Before choosing an instrument, pupils can become familiar with the sound and sight of several. Ideally, this will be through high-quality live performances, perhaps by teachers, concert performers, parents, secondary pupils, or primary pupils. Groups should be small enough for pupils to be close to the instrument, and have a chance to ask questions. Recordings combined with pictures are a poor alternative to live performance.

2. Do not place too much weight on whether a child can initially make a pleasant sound on an instrument

Instrument teachers faced with the problem of selecting a few pupils from a large number who want lessons sometimes resort to passing an instrument round, and seeing who can make the best sound. This is successful selection in the sense that the number of pupils left is reduced, but a correlation between an initial ability to play an instrument and ultimate achievement, for instance, is unproven. In fact, one can find many counter-examples—professional horn players who spent their first three lessons unable to produce a note, for example. Pupils can be taught to blow wind and brass instruments; those who can do so initially simply have a head start, and will be easier for the teacher to teach in the first instance. Consequently, if pupils are permitted to try to play instruments as part of the familiarization stage suggested above, those who produce only weird sounds, or even no sounds at all, should be reminded that tuition could help to remedy this.

3. Beware of physical suitability, personality, and gender stereotypes

There is a mythology associated with the gender, personality, and physical attributes which make pupils suitable, or unsuitable, to play particular instruments. Like most mythology, some of it has been around a long time. As long ago as 1935, two Americans, Charles Lamp and Noel Keys (1935), were prompted to investigate some supposed correlations between physical attributes and instrumental achievement. Teachers told the researchers that lip-thickness is relevant to pupils' most appropriate choice of brass instrument: pupils should choose instruments with a mouthpiece size corresponding to the thickness of their lips. Thus thin-lipped pupils should choose instruments such as horns and trumpets, whilst those with thick lips should choose instruments such as trombones and tubas. This view is presumably based on the notion that thick lips will vibrate better at the lower frequencies, that is, lower notes, played by trombones and tubas. Teachers also told Lamp and Keys that string players need long fingers, and wind players need even teeth. Subsequent investigation of the relationship between pupils' progress on instruments, and their possession of supposedly advantageous physical attributes, did not confirm these hypotheses.[1] Indeed the boy with the thinnest lips, and the boy with the thickest lips, both went on to become proficient French horn players. Over 50 years later, we still sometimes find physical characteristics such as these being used to select pupils for instruments. Early in the 1980s (Mills 1983) I interviewed 50 instrument teachers to find out what physical attributes each thought predicted success on the instruments on which they gave lessons. I found that some of the assumptions held by the teachers in Lamp and Keys' investigation are still commonly held. In addition, teachers explained why they believe that some other physical attributes are important. For instance, some bassoon teachers believe that bassoonists need particularly even front teeth because of the way in which the bassoon double reed is held. Some percussion teachers believe that percussionists need particularly fine motor coordination because of the high control of fine movement required during the performance of intricate rhythms. A handful of teachers declined to teach pupils who had supposedly undesirable physical attributes. But amongst other teachers' pupils I found high-flying instrumentalists with all sorts of supposedly undesirable features: short-armed trombonists, thick-lipped trumpeters, left-handed cellists, thin-lipped oboists, buck-teethed bassoonists, clumsy percussionists, and so on. As in selection by passing an instrument round, selection by physical attribute achieves the desired purpose of reducing the number of pupils present, but it has little to do with selection of pupils with high potential for achievement.

I have found (Mills 1988b) a physical characteristic that predicts instrumental achievement better than any of the criteria which the teachers were using: left-hand digital formula. To assess yours, place your left hand palm down on a flat surface, with your fingers together. Note whether your index finger or your ring finger reaches further up your middle finger. If your ring finger reaches further

---

[1] The correlation between achievement on brass instruments and appropriateness of mouthpiece size is only small ($r = 0.28 \pm 0.088$). The correlation between finger length and achievement on the violin is lower still ($r = 0.17 \pm 0.09$). In fact it is much the same as the violinists' result for teeth-evenness—not a characteristic we would expect to be relevant to violinists!

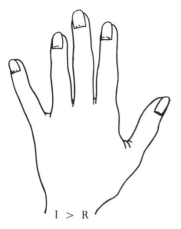 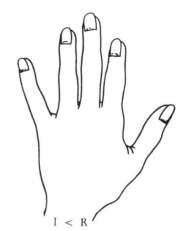

I > R   I < R

Fig. 8 Left-hand digital formula.

you have an I < R formula, along with about 70 per cent of the general population. Otherwise, you have the less usual I > R formula (see Fig. 8). I compared the left-hand digital formula of some accomplished instrumentalists[2] with that of a general population. Hardly any of the violin or viola players had the I > R formula. Yet a majority of the other performers had the unusual I > R formula.

Digital formula is not customarily used in any type of musical selection. I came across it in an anatomy textbook (Jones 1941), not a music textbook. It is reasonable to suppose that the distribution of digital formula in pupils starting lessons on any instrument will be much the same as in the general population. It seems, though, that digital formula is predisposing some pupils towards success; the I < R formula benefits violinists and viola players, and the I > R formula promotes success on other orchestral instruments. Yet it would be preposterous to suggest that digital formula should become part of any selection procedure, for two main reasons:

◆ We do not know whether the apparent relationship between formula and success is inevitable, or the result of insensitive teaching. Think, for instance, of the left-hand positions which violinists of differing digital formula must adopt in order to rest all their left-hand fingertips on a string simultaneously. Much string technique is learnt by copying a teacher. If the teacher has an I < R formula, but has not noticed that a pupil has an I > R formula, is copying likely to result in the pupil developing a useful left-hand technique?

---

[2] Some of the instrumentalists were students at a specialist music school. The remainder were receiving professional training as musicians.

♦ Some people without the preferred formula are succeeding. So even if the general association between formula and success is nothing to do with teaching, screening according to digital formula would result in some potential professional musicians being denied lessons.

There is just one occasion on which the physical attributes of normal pupils might render them unsuitable to start some instruments: when they are insufficiently physically mature, that is, still too small. A child may have too small a hand span to be able to stretch between the keys on a clarinet, for instance. But these occasions are infrequent. Violins and cellos can be obtained in a variety of sizes to suit pupils from the age of around 3 onwards. Violins can be used as small violas, and cellos can be strung as small double basses. A trombonist just unable to reach the lowest, seventh, position can avoid using it until she or he has grown a little. Flutes with U-shaped tubes, suitable for pupils not able to reach the full length of a standard flute, are occasionally seen.

Decisions that a child cannot start an instrument because of small size are only temporary; pupils do eventually grow. All standard instruments are suitable for large and small adults. The conductor Neville Marriner may, or may not, have been serious when he said that 'only really very tall conductors can deal adequately with slow music'. But orchestras include large piccolo players and small double-bass players who demonstrate a formidable technique in fast music, slow music, and that which lies between.

We have seen the dangers in over-generalizing findings that the majority of successful performers of any instrument have particular physical attributes. The same is true for attributes of personality. Although the personality structure of musicians has been investigated in a serious and sustained manner (Kemp 1996), potential pupils may occasionally be allocated to instruments on the basis of evidence scarcely above the level of the following orchestral clarinettist's summary of the orchestra: 'the brass are drinkers, the wind are thinkers, and the strings are stinkers', (Davies 1978: 203). Personality stereotyping abounds in music. The social structure of orchestras seems to reinforce it. But it has yet to be proved that any measured difference in the personality of different categories of successful instrumentalists is present at the start of tuition, rather than arising during it, perhaps through contact with the stereotyping.

In *The Right Instrument for Your Child*, Atarah Ben-Tovim and Douglas Boyd (Ben-Tovim and Boyd 1985) describe an instrument selection system that is intended to help parents choose the instrument to which their child is best suited. This system includes personality assessment—parents assess whether the personality of their child matches that of some successful young performers whom Ben-Tovim and Boyd have observed. Again, we see unjustified generalization of attributes. If Ben-Tovim and Boyd have observed that most successful young horn players 'prefer to relate to small groups and usually have just one or two close friends', should we really steer particularly popular pupils towards another instrument? Ben-Tovim and Boyd's statements about personality seem closely related to the role of the instrument concerned in the classical symphony orchestra. For instance, in the symphony orchestra, large numbers of first and second violins play the same part. Thus it might be thought that violinists need sheep-like characteristics. And, Ben-Tovim and Boyd do indeed tell us that the violin is suitable for 'quietly behaved pupils' with 'no outlet for boisterousness or exuberance'. Orchestral trumpeters have their own, frequently prominent, part. Thus, Ben-Tovim and Boyd tell us that the trumpet is suitable for the 'individualist' with 'prima donna temperament'. The list continues. Symphony orchestras include plenty of extrovert violinists who are not in the throes of a personality crisis. One of the attributes of all successful violinists must surely be that they like some of the sounds made by violins. Yet pupils' preference amongst instrument sounds forms no part of Ben-Tovim and Boyd's method. In fact, the child does not seem to be in on the choice at all.

There is no evidence that pupils of either gender are predisposed towards success on any instrument. Yet it is common knowledge that some instruments are considered—by parents and pupils—to be more suitable for boys than girls, and vice versa. Girls tend to choose small, high-pitched orchestral instruments, boys tend to choose the large, low-pitched ones. There is no practical reason for this.[3] Girls are, clearly, capable of carrying and holding large instruments. Indeed, at the age at which tuition usually starts, around 11, girls are often bigger and stronger than boys. And as boys usually start instrument tuition before their voices change, they cannot be choosing low-pitched instruments because of a correspondence with their own vocal range.[4] Susan O'Neill found a similar list of preferences in more recent work in the UK (Mills 2007: 75).

---

[3] Occasionally, one finds a piece of music that is not playable by both men and women. In Luciano Berio's *Sequenza V*, written for solo trombone in 1966, the trombonist has to sing notes outside the female vocal range into his trombone. The existence of this piece is not enough to render the trombone only suitable for men, as many successful women trombonists have shown.

[4] Leontiev (1969), amongst others, has shown that pitch discrimination is often more accurate within the vocal range, because of the possibility of sub-vocalization. Thus, it might be argued that men are likely to play low instruments better in tune. Yet Leontiev showed that ability to discriminate pitch finely within the vocal range could be extended beyond it. I am sure that I am not alone in finding that my ability to tune children's cellos, for instance, has improved with practice.

The association of gender with instruments is not just a British problem. Harold Abeles and Susan Porter (1978) found, in the USA, that parents' choice of instruments for sons differed from that for daughters. Adults were given eight instruments to choose from. Clarinets, flutes, and violins were preferred for daughters, whilst drums, trombones, and trumpets were preferred for sons, and the cello and saxophone were without significant gender association. The pupils' personal preferences for the instruments of the appropriate gender association were developing by the age of 7, and stable by the age of 9. Philip Griswold and Denise Chroback (1981) replicated much of this investigation. Their experimental evidence added harps, piccolos, glockenspiels, cellos, pianos, French horns, and oboes to the feminine list, and guitars, cymbals, saxophones, double basses, and tubas to the masculine list.

Gender stereotyping is to be deplored because it decreases the choice of instruments available to both boys and girls. What can we do to help remove it, or at least avoid reinforcing it? The last stage of Abeles and Porter's investigation provides a clue. They investigated the effect on pupils' gender associations of different methods of presenting the instruments and found, not surprisingly, that photographs of girls playing 'feminine' instruments and boys playing 'masculine' instruments were part of the problem, particularly for boys. So it seems likely that we could reduce the gender association of instruments through positive presentation of performers of the 'wrong' sex for their instrument. Take a look at the music books in your class library, and the music posters on your classroom walls, and consider removing any that reinforce stereotypes. But do not go over the top. The odd holiday postcard from Wales displaying a woman with a large black hat playing a harp will not, I think, do lasting harm to pupils. And I would not recommend following Abeles and Porter's findings concerning boys' particular susceptibility to pictorial gender associations to a logical conclusion of presenting pictures of males playing everything. I recall a pupils' book in which males play all the orchestral instruments, whilst the females are confined to blowing across bottles, and playing plastic recorders. This does not do much for the professional aspirations of female musicians.

As a teacher in a comprehensive school in the heart of brass band land, I found that whilst roughly even numbers of girls and boys were interested in playing the cornet and trumpet, no girls wanted to take up the trombone. I attempted to resolve this through role modelling: I took up the trombone myself. The scale of the gender bias concerning trombones in this locality became apparent when I made my debut at a school concert. As I walked onto the platform carrying a trombone, a portion of the audience dissolved into laughter, and that was before I played anything. My subsequent rendition of a bass line to *Raindrops Keep Falling on My Head* was, not surprisingly, insufficient to remove gender stereotyping overnight. But female trumpeters started to take my trombone away for a bit of surreptitious lunchtime practice. It did seem that role modelling was helpful, even at this late, secondary, age.

4.   Consider apparent motivation, but do not overrate it

We would probably all agree that a child will not receive much benefit from instrument lessons unless she or he is motivated to want to play the instrument. The problem is that motivation can be ill-informed. A child over the moon about the prospect of cello lessons may not have understood—however many times you have told him—that learning to play any instrument is a slow business. A child who has understood this may appear less motivated. A certain amount of motivation is essential, but using it as the sole means of selection can result in serious, thoughtful, pupils being left out. In selection systems where a class teacher works in partnership with an instrument teacher, the class teacher is often in the better position to assess the significance of an individual's motivation.

Working in Australia, Gary McPherson (2000) interviewed pupils who were shortly to begin instrumental lessons, and discovered that those who thought that they would be learning for only a few months generally did so. It is useful for teachers to know that pupils sometimes have such low expectations of themselves. I would suggest that we respond to this research by working to raise pupils' expectations of themselves, and giving them the joy in playing that leads to them wanting to continue it for ever.

It is sometimes assumed that motivation towards instrument lessons is a quality that a child either has or lacks. Thus a child who gives up lessons on the violin, for instance, may be deemed to lack motivation, and denied flute lessons. In fact, motivation towards any activity is multi-faceted. In the case of instrument lessons, it is influenced by the instrument chosen, the teacher, and style of teaching, the social dynamic of the group of pupils, and so on. In other words, a child who gives up lessons on an instrument is not destined to give up any other instrument that is offered. Amongst a sample of 46 professional orchestral musicians (Mills 1985), I found four who had first taken lessons on an orchestral instrument significantly different from the one they were employed to play. A trumpeter and a trombonist had both started with violin lessons. A clarinettist had started with the flute. A tuba player had started with the trombone. In addition, there were some more usual transfers: violinists had become viola players, and cellists had transferred to the double bass. In other words, a decision not to persevere with one instrument does not necessarily imply a general lack of ability to persevere.

5. **Think carefully about any assessment you want to make of 'musical ability'**

Selection for instruments sometimes includes some form of assessment of 'musical ability'. Often, this is based on the child's ability to sing in tune. This is a highly dubious predictor of any sort of ability. The assessor is really interested in whether the child can 'hear in tune', yet a child who can hear fine differences in pitch may still lack the vocal control to sing a simple song in tune. In other words, a child who sings in tune probably has fine pitch discrimination, but the converse is not true. Other teacher-designed ability tests include aural tests administered from the piano. A teacher may play a chord, and then ask pupils how many notes it contains, for instance. There are two main problems in this. First, pupils already familiar with the sound of a piano will be at an advantage. Second, the ability to count the number of notes in a chord is not a major component of performing. To what extent can the teacher be certain that the ability to count the number of notes in a chord is indicative of any more general ability? In other words, to what extent is this test a valid predictor of any wider ability?

How can you avoid these problems? If you wish to include assessment of pupils' musical ability in your selection procedure, you can use a published test, such as my *Group Tests of Musical Abilities* (Mills 1988a). Published tests can offer several advantages over home-made tests. First, they may already have been tried out with a large sample of pupils. Second, an attempt may have been made to minimize the probably inevitable advantage given to pupils with extensive musical background. Third, the extent to which the tests predict achievement on instruments may have been investigated. Supporting documentation for tests enables you to determine their suitability for your particular purposes.

My view is that pupils' results in tests should always be interpreted positively. They should not be used to discourage pupils from taking lessons. The best way of finding out whether a child will benefit from trumpet lessons is to give him some and see what happens. However, test results can lead to your recognition of some able pupils of whom you were previously unaware. Perhaps they are quiet pupils who do not customarily make their presence felt at all. Perhaps they are pupils who have not displayed particular musical behaviour; they could dislike singing, or may not sing in tune. A high-scoring child might be offered some special encouragement to start lessons.

Should all pupils be tested as a matter of course? I see little purpose in this. But if a decision needs to be made about a child's musical future, a test score can provide a piece of evidence to be considered alongside that which a teacher already has at her disposal.

6. **Think carefully about the extent to which you wish to consider factors concerned with home background and academic attainment**

It is well known that factors that predispose pupils towards academic success, such as high measured intelligence and positive parental support, also correlate with musical attainment. Desmond Sergeant and Gillian Thatcher (1974) found that pupils with high measured intelligence and social status tend to score better in musical ability tests. Because of the tradition of equating effective selection for instrument tuition with low wastage, such fortunate pupils are often given priority when places for instrument lessons are scarce. My view is that this is wrong. There are no perfect correlations between musical attainment and social or academic factors. Some pupils from the most depressive social circumstances become successful musicians. And there are many professional musicians with few formal academic qualifications. If anything, I would argue for pupils in less favourable circumstances to be given preferential treatment. They are probably less likely to have parents able or willing to provide instrument lessons outside school. As teachers, we try to provide a primary education that enables pupils to achieve their potential, regardless of their social background or ability. Why should instrument lessons be any different?

School music and secondary teachers

There was a time when primary/secondary liaison in music was almost unheard of. The range of musical experience of pupils entering a particular secondary school was often vast. Much of the variation could be attributed to the differing status of music within the feeder, or partner, schools. Some secondary teachers responded imaginatively to the range of initial experience. Others reacted by taking everyone back to what they regarded as the beginning, thus boring some pupils through repetition. A further group organized class music as a form of entertainment, rather than a progressive course. Primary schools and secondary schools viewed themselves as autonomous; nothing much happened to remedy mismatch, or to find a more constructive way of dealing with it.

With more positive attitudes to primary/secondary liaison, secondary music teachers have sometimes found themselves with some time available to teach in one or more of their partner schools. Unfortunately, this sort of teaching has sometimes been a hit-and-run, top-down, affair, with secondary teachers arriving to teach primary pupils whatever it is that the secondary teachers want them to know when they change school. The content of these secondary teachers' lessons was not always related to anything else that the pupils were doing, and was sometimes conveyed in a specialist way almost guaranteed to intimidate every primary teacher without a music degree. At its worst, this style of liaison actually decreased the amount of music teaching and learning taking place in the primary school.

Thanks partly to the introduction of the National Curriculum, and the Early Years Foundation Stage Curriculum, there is now much greater awareness that music in school is, at the very least, a 4 to 14 process. This has opened the door to more constructive pooling of the staffing of secondary and primary schools. Primary and secondary teachers learn from each other. Though secondary music teachers, as trained music specialists, often have more in the way of formal music qualifications, there is often much they can learn about music education from primary teachers and pupils: the high expectations that can be set, the almost general enthusiasm for music of primary pupils, the possibilities of informal modes of teaching, the relationship between music and the remainder of the curriculum, and so on. More than ever before, secondary teachers need to find out about the musical achievements of their intake, so that they can build on them. They can acquire much information from reports. But first-hand observation, too, is helpful. Seeing and hearing primary pupils at work helps secondary teachers set expectations that are high enough, and ensure that the secondary curriculum reinforces, and does not simply repeat, the primary curriculum. Sadly, secondary teachers are more likely to underestimate than overestimate work they have not seen. That does pupils no good, and does not add to the musical reputation of the primary school.

Primary and secondary schools are, of course, very busy places. But perhaps you could encourage a couple of secondary music teachers to visit your school—to join your pupils composing, singing, and playing, and encourage them to discuss some pupils' work with the pupils themselves.

A school staff for music

A school staff for music includes all the teachers: consultants, class teachers, teaching assistants, visiting teachers and artists, the headteacher. It may also include secondary teachers, parents, and other members of the community. Though a music curriculum leader may take prime responsibility for writing a music curriculum document, everyone is involved in its design and implementation.

Teachers have individual differences in their musical interests. No two teachers working in the same school will interpret their school music curriculum document in exactly the same way. The best sort of music curriculum document secures progression whilst capitalizing on the diversity of teachers' musical experience.

One year, a child may be in the class of a teacher who chooses to play and perform a lot of rap. The next year, there may be more Ravel. The year after, it may be mainly ragtime. One year, most singing may be unaccompanied. The next year, the piano may be used more. The third year may be the year of the guitar. A teacher who is a visual artist may favour the use of visual stimuli for composing, whereas another teacher may make more extensive use of poetry or ICT. The mathematics curriculum leader may place emphasis on pattern in music. The PE teacher may see close links between music and dance. Another teacher may feel more comfortable teaching music as a self-contained subject. Some teachers will have strong personal musical interests which they want to share with pupils. Others will prefer to start by considering the music that pupils bring with them from their community, or the musical ideas conveyed by the school or home environment. This range of interest and emphasis is a source of great strength to a school. A staff that is able to pool all this can offer pupils a music programme much richer than one person could ever supply. Pupils continually become aware of new dimensions of music, and new emphases within music-making. They have first-hand experience of the coexistence of different musical traditions, and plenty of material from which to develop their personal musical taste.

Within a school staff for music, teachers can be encouraged to develop and build on their musical strengths. They also learn from each other. Confident teachers help less confident teachers to develop as music teachers. In return, they learn much from those they help. By finding approaches to teaching that class teachers feel ready to tackle, consultants develop their own repertoire of teaching skills. Through teaching their colleagues music skills, more confident teachers become better equipped to teach them to pupils. Very few adults who are fluent music readers, for instance, can remember learning to read music themselves. Teaching an adult learner who is able to articulate his or her difficulties can sometimes lead to a more consistent approach with pupils. But there is also much more to be learnt from class teachers: the differing responses of individuals to the same piece of music, the open response of teachers who have not come to view some sorts of music as 'good' and others as 'bad', a way of talking about music that is free of technical jargon. Music teaching is a cooperative enterprise in which pupils gain from teachers, and teachers gain from each other.

Suggestions for further reading

DES (1985). *Curriculum Matters 4: Music from 5 to 16*. London: HMSO.

Glover, J. (2000). *Children Composing 4–14*. London: RoutledgeFalmer.

—— and Young, S. (1999). *Primary Music: Later Years*. London: Falmer.

Hennessy, S. (1995). *Music 7–11: Developing Primary Teaching Skills*. London: Routledge.

—— (1998). *Coordinating Music across the Primary School*. London: Falmer.

Mills, J. (2005). *Music in the School*. Oxford: Oxford University Press.

—— (2007). *Instrumental Teaching*. Oxford: Oxford University Press.

Paynter, J. (1992). *Sound and Structure*. Cambridge: Cambridge University Press.

Pound, L., and Harrison, D. (2003). *Supporting Musical Development in the Early Years*. Buckingham: Open University Press.

Young, S. (2008) *Music 3–5*. London: *Nursery World*/Routledge.

—— and Glover, J. (1998). *Music in the Early Years*. London: Falmer.

References

Abeles, H. F., and Porter, S. Y. (1978). 'The Sex-Stereotyping of Musical Instruments', *Journal of Research in Music Education* 26: 65–75.

Addison, R. (1988). 'Beyond Music'. In W. Salaman and J. Mills (eds), *Challenging Assumptions: New Perspectives in the Education of Music Teachers*. Exeter: University of Exeter School of Education.

APMT (1988). *Music Therapy in the Education Service: A Consultation Document*. APMT.

Arnold, J. (1984). 'Music and Integrated Arts Studies'. In P. Farmer (ed.), *Music in Practice*. Oxford: Oxford University Press.

Barrett, M. (2005a). 'Musical Communication and Children's Communities of Musical Practice'. In D. Miell, R. MacDonald, and D. J. Hargreaves (eds), *Musical Communication*. Oxford: Oxford University Press.

—— (2005b). 'Children's Communities of Musical Practice: Some Socio-cultural Implications of a Systems View of Creativity in Music Education. In D. J. Elliott (ed.), *Praxial Music Education*. Oxford: Oxford University Press.

Bennett, N., and Carré, C. (1993). *Learning to Teach*. London: Routledge.

Bentley, A. (1966). *Musical Ability in Children and its Measurement*. London: Harrap.

—— (1968). *'Monotones'—a Comparison with 'Normal' Singers*. London: Novello.

Ben-Tovim, A., and Boyd, D. (1985). *The Right Instrument for your Child*. London: Gollancz.

Betjeman, J. (1960). *Summoned by Bells*. London: John Murray.

Bridger, W. (1961). 'Sensory Habituation and Discrimination in the Human Neonate', *American Journal of Psychiatry* 117: 991–6.

Bryant, P., and Bradley, L. (1985). *Children's Reading Problems*. Oxford: Blackwell.

Buckton, R. (1988). 'Vocal Accuracy of Young Children—a New Zealand Survey'. In A. E. Kemp (ed.), *Research in Music Education: A Festschrift for Arnold Bentley*. Reading: International Society for Music Education.

Bunting, R. (1977). 'The Common Language of Music'. In *Music in the Secondary School Curriculum*, Working Paper 6, York University.

Burt, R. (2007). 'Preschool Children's Emotional Responses to Music: A Window into Learning in the Early Years'. In K. Smithrim and R. Upitis (eds), *Listen to their Voices: Research and Practice in Early Childhood Music*. Toronto: Canadian Music Educators' Association, 126–39.

CACE (1967). *Children and their Primary Schools* (Plowden Report). London: HMSO.

Cage, J. (1962). *Silence: Letters and Writings*. London: Calder and Boyars.

Campbell, P. S. (1998). *Songs in their Heads: Music and its Meaning in Children's Lives*. New York: Oxford University Press.

Carson Turner, B. (ed.) (1988). *Hullabaloo-balay*. Basingstoke: Macmillan.

Cleall, C. (1970). *Voice Production in Choral Technique*. London: Novello.

Cornford, F. M. (1969). *The Republic of Plato*. Oxford: Oxford University Press.

Corredor, J. M. (1956). *Conversations with Casals*. London: Hutchinson.

Crowther, R., and Durkin, K. (1982). 'Research Overview: Language in Music Education', *Psychology of Music* 10/1: 59–60.

Davies, C. (1986). 'Say it till a Song Comes (Reflections on Songs Invented by Children 3–13)', *British Journal of Music Education* 3/3: 279–93.

—— (1992). 'Listen to my Song: A Study of Songs Invented by Children Aged 5 to 7 Years', *British Journal of Music Education* 9/1: 19–48.

Davies, J. B. (1978). *The Psychology of Music*. London: Hutchinson.

DES (1978). *Primary Education in England: A Survey of HM Inspectors of Schools*. London: HMSO.

—— (1982). *Education 5 to 9: An Illustrative Survey of 80 First Schools in England*. London: HMSO.

—— (1985). *Curriculum Matters 4: Music from 5 to 16*. London: HMSO.

—— (1991a). *Mathematics in the National Curriculum*. London: HMSO.

—— (1991b). *Science in the National Curriculum*. London: HMSO.

—— (1992). *Music in the National Curriculum (England)*. London, HMSO.

DfEE and QCA (1999a). *Music: The National Curriculum for England*. London: HMSO.

DfEE and QCA (1999b). *Science: The National Curriculum for England*. London: HMSO.

DfEE and QCA (1999c). *English: The National Curriculum for England*. London, HMSO.

Devon County Council (1988). *Music-Lines*. Exeter: Devon County Council.

Gadsby, D., and Harrop, B. (2002). *Flying a Round*, 2nd edn, London: A and C. Black.

Gardner, H., and Winner, E. (1982). 'First Intimations of Artistry'. In S. Strauss and S. Stavy (eds), *U-Shaped Behavioural Growth*. New York: Academic Press.

Glover, J., and Young, S. (1999). *Primary Music: Later Years*. London: Falmer.

Griswold, P. A., and Chroback, D. A. (1981). 'Sex-Role Associations of Music Instruments and Occupations by Gender and Major', *Journal of Research in Music Education* 29/1: 57–62.

Hargreaves, D. J. (1986). *The Developmental Psychology of Music*. Cambridge: Cambridge University Press.

Igaga, J. M., and Versey, J. (1977). 'Cultural Differences in Rhythmic Perception', *Psychology of Music* 5/1: 23–7.

—— (1978). 'Cultural Differences in Rhythmic Performance', *Psychology of Music* 6/1: 61–4.

Jones, F. W. (1941). *The Principles of Anatomy as Seen in the Hand*. London. Ballière and Cox.

Jørgensen, H. (2001). 'Instrumental Learning: Is an Early Start a Key to Success?' *British Journal of Music Education* 18/3: 227–39.

Keller, H. (1987). *Criticism*. London: Faber and Faber.

Kemp, A. E. (1996). *The Musical Temperament: Psychology and Personality of Musicians*. Oxford: Oxford University Press.

Lamp, C. J., and Keys, N. (1935). 'Can Aptitude for Specific Musical Instruments be Predicted?' *American Journal of Educational Psychology* 26: 587–96.

Leontiev, O. (1969). 'On the Biological and Social Aspects of Human Development: The Training of Auditory Ability'. In M. Cole and I. Matzman (eds), *A Handbook of Contemporary Soviet Psychology*. New York: Basic Books.

Letwin, O. (1987). 'Testing Issues', *Times Educational Supplement* (18 Sept.): 112.

Lloyd, L. (2007). 'Composition Inspired by Ligeti', *National Association of Music Educators Magazine* 20: 8–9.

Loane, B. (1984). 'Thinking about Children's Composition', *British Journal of Music Education* 1/3: 205–32.

McPherson, G. (2000). 'Commitment and Practice: Key Ingredients for Achievement during the Early Stages of Learning a Musical Instrument', *Bulletin of the Council for Research in Music Education* 147: 122–7.

—— (ed.) (2006). *The Child as Musician.* Oxford: Oxford University Press.

Malbran, S., and Furno, S. (1987). 'Objective Test for Songs', *Bulletin of the Council for Research in Music Education* 91: 110–18.

Mang, E. (2001). 'Intermediate Vocalizations: An Investigation of the Boundary between Speech and Songs in Young Children's Vocalizations', *Bulletin of the Council for Research in Music Education* 147: 116–21.

Marsh, K., and Young, S. (2006). 'Musical Play'. In G. McPherson (ed.), *The Child as Musician.* Oxford: Oxford University Press.

Marshall, S. (1963). *An Experiment in Education.* Cambridge: Cambridge University Press.

Mawbey, W. E. (1973). 'Wastage from Instrumental Classes in School', *Psychology of Music* 1/1: 33–43.

Mills, J. (1983). 'Identifying Potential Orchestral Musicians'. D.Phil. thesis, Oxford University.

—— (1985). 'Gifted Instrumentalists: How Can We Recognise Them?' *British Journal of Music Education* 2/1: 39–49.

—— (1988a). *Group Tests of Musical Abilities: Teacher's Guide and Recorded Test.* Windsor, NFER–Nelson.

—— (1988b). 'Tips for Teachers as Traps: An Example from Instrumental Tuition'. In W. Salaman and J. Mills (eds), *Challenging Assumptions: New Perspectives in the Education of Music Teachers.* Exeter: University of Exeter School of Education.

—— (1989a). 'Developing Listening through Composing', *Music Teacher* (March): 9–11.

—— (1989b). 'Generalist Primary Teachers of Music: A Problem of Confidence', *British Journal of Music Education* 6/2: 125–38.

—— (1995/6). 'Primary Student Teachers as Musicians', *Bulletin for the Council for Research in Music Education* 127: 122–6.

—— (1996). 'Starting at Secondary School', *British Journal of Music Education* 13: 5–14.

—— (1997). 'Knowing the Subject versus Knowing the Child: Striking the Right Balance for Children aged 7–11 Years', *Research Studies in Music Education* 9: 29–35.

—— (1998). 'Response to Katie Overy's Paper, "Can Music Really 'Improve' the Mind?" ' *Psychology of Music* 26/2: 204–5.

—— (2004). 'Perspectives', *Link* 2: 50.

—— (2005). *Music in the School.* Oxford: Oxford University Press.

—— (2007). *Instrumental Teaching.* Oxford: Oxford University Press.

—— and O'Neill, S. A. (2002). 'Children as Inspectors? Evaluating School Music Provision for Children Aged 10–11 Years', *British Journal of Music Education* 19/3: 285–302.

Moog, H. (1976). *The Musical Experience of the Pre-school Child,* trans. Claudia Clarke. London: Schott.

Morley, T. (1952). *A Plaine and Easie Introduction to Practicalle Musicke.* London: Dent.

National Curriculum Council (1989). *A Framework for the Primary Curriculum.* National Curriculum Council, York.

Opie, I., and Opie, P. (1985). *The Singing Game*. Oxford: Oxford University Press.

Overy, K. (1998). 'Can Music Really "Improve" the Mind?' *Psychology of Music* 26/1: 97–9.

Parncutt, R., and McPherson, G. (eds) (2002). *The Science and Psychology of Music Performance*. Oxford: Oxford University Press.

Paynter, J. (1972). *The Space Dragon of Galatar*. London: Universal Edition.

—— (1982). *Music in the Secondary School Curriculum*. Cambridge: Cambridge University Press.

—— (1992). *Sound and Structure*. Cambridge: Cambridge University Press.

—— and Aston, P. (1970). *Sound and Silence*. Cambridge: Cambridge University Press.

Piaget, J. (1951). *Play, Dreams and Imitation in Childhood*. London: Routledge and Kegan Paul.

Pound, L., and Harrison, D. (2003). *Supporting Musical Development in the Early Years*. Buckingham: Open University Press.

Primary Schools Research and Development Group (1983). *Curriculum Responsibility and the Use of Teacher Expertise in the Primary School*. Birmingham: University of Birmingham School of Education.

Ross, M. (1984). *The Aesthetic Impulse*. Oxford: Pergamon Press.

Salaman, W. (1988). 'Personalities in World Music Education No.7—John Paynter', *International Journal of Music Education* 12: 28–32.

Seashore, C. E. (1938). *The Psychology of Music*. London: McGraw-Hill.

Sergeant, D. C., and Thatcher, G. (1974). 'Intelligence, Social Status, and Musical Abilities', *Psychology of Music* 2/2: 32–57.

Shuter-Dyson, R., and Gabriel, C. (1981). *The Psychology of Musical Ability*, 2nd edn, London: Methuen.

Spychiger, M., *et al.* (1993). *Music Makes the School*. Essen: Verlag Blaue Eule.

Sundin, B. (1998). 'Musical Creativity in the First Six Years: A Research Project in Retrospect'. In B. Sundin, G. McPherson, and G. Folkestad (eds), *Children Composing*. Malmö: Malmö Academy of Music.

Swanwick, K. (1979). *A Basis for Music Education*. Windsor: NFER/Nelson.

—— (1988). *Music, Mind and Education*. London, Routledge.

—— and Tillman, J. (1986). 'The Sequence of Musical Development: A Study of Children's Composition', *British Journal of Music Education* 3/3: 305–39.

Taylor, S. (1973). 'Musical Development of Children Aged Seven to Eleven', *Psychology of Music* 1/1: 44–9.

Thompson, D., and Baxter, K. (1978). *Pompaleerie Jig*. London: Arnold-Wheaton.

Tillman, J. (1988). 'Music in the Primary School and the National Curriculum'. In W. Salaman and J. Mills (eds), *Challenging Assumptions: New Perspectives in the Education of Music Teachers*. Exeter: University of Exeter School of Education.

Trehub, S. E. (2006). 'Infants as Musical Connoisseurs'. In G. McPherson (ed.), *The Child as Musician*. Oxford: Oxford University Press.

Untermeyer, L. (ed.) (1961). *The Golden Treasury of Poetry*. London: Collins.

Vulliamy, G., and Lee, E. (1976). *Pop Music in School*. Cambridge: Cambridge University Press.

Welch, G. (1979). 'Vocal Range and Poor Pitch Singing', *Psychology of Music* 7/2: 13–31.

Wisbey, A. (1980). *Music as the Source of Learning*. Lancaster: MTP.

—— (1981). *Learn to Sing to Learn to Read*. London: BBC.

Wishart, T. (1975). *Sounds Fun*. London: Schools Council Publications.

Young, S., and Glover, J. (1998). *Music in the Early Years*. London: Falmer.

Index

This index is in letter-by-letter order. Page references in *italics* indicate figures; those in **bold** indicate photos.